"Powerful, poignant and pert[...] both mind and spirit. As read[...] wholeheartedly commend it."

Revd John Glass, General Superintendant, Elim

"Powerfully and prophetically challenges the church to see this as an age of opportunity – to confidently contend for the faith and boldly offer the unbelievable gospel as the hope for the world."

Revd Simon Ponsonby, Pastor of Theology, St Aldates Oxford

"*Unbelievable* has strengthened my belief and given me confidence, as well as an excitement and new vigour to share my faith with others."

Fiona Castle OBE

"In exploring the Apostles' Creed, *Unbelievable* roots us in the great truths of Scripture and in this we find a fresh confidence in the amazing God we serve and His purposes in the world."

Steve Clifford, General Director, Evangelical Alliance

"Immensely accessible and helpful. I felt excitement burning in my heart as I imagined what the confident church could be, by the unfathomable Father, in the unbeatable Son and through the unstoppable Spirit. I'm a believer."

Abby Guinness, Spring Harvest Event Director

"A call to regain a fully biblical faith, viewed through the lens of the Apostles' Creed. A passionate call to authentic believing and living. An irresistible call to a confident yet humble faith in a gospel that still has the power to change the world!"

Stephen Gaukroger, Director, Clarion Trust International

"Deeply challenges and encourages. The Gospel is the hope for the world and Malcolm's wonderfully written book gives every Christian greater confidence to share it."

Gavin Calver, National Director, Youth for Christ

"God-honouring; Christ-centred; Holy Spirit-inspired; Bible-based; robust; intrusive; and demanding some kind of response. If what Malcolm writes here is true, life must become forever different."

Jim Graham, Pastor Emeritus, Gold Hill Baptist Church

"A brilliant exposition. Biblical, readable, radical and practical – I loved it!"

Lyndon Bowring, Executive Chairman, CARE

"Simply, comprehensively, winsomely and compassionately, Malcolm Duncan leads us through an ancient Creed that educates our minds, illuminates our hearts, and presents us with a vision of an unfathomable, unbeatable, unstoppable God."

Dr Steve Brady, Principal, Moorlands College, Christchurch

"The author has done a commendable job in bringing us back to solid theology at a time the church would be wise to be more and more interested in sound teaching."

Dr R. T. Kendall

UNBELIEVABLE

CONFIDENT FAITH IN A SCEPTICAL WORLD

MALCOLM DUNCAN

MONARCH
BOOKS

Oxford, UK & Grand Rapids, Michigan, USA

Published by Monarch Books, an imprint of Lion Hudson plc
Wilkinson House, Jordan Hill Road, Oxford OX2 8DR, England
Email: monarch@lionhudson.com
www.lionhudson.com/monarch
and by Elevation (an imprint of the Memralife Group)
Memralife Group, 14 Horsted Square, Uckfield, East Sussex TN22 1QG
Tel: +44 (0)1825 746530; Fax +44 (0)1825 748899;
www.elevationmusic.com

ISBN 978 0 85721 534 5
e-ISBN 978 0 85721 535 2

First edition 2014

Acknowledgments

Unless otherwise stated Scripture quotations taken from the New Revised Standard Version of the Bible, Anglicized Edition, copyright © 1989, 1995 by the Division of Christian Education of the National Council of the Churches of Christ in the United States of America, and are used by permission. All rights reserved. Scripture quotations marked "NIV" taken from the Holy Bible, New International Version Anglicized. Copyright © 1979, 1984, 2011 Biblica, formerly International Bible Society. Used by permission of Hodder & Stoughton Ltd, an Hachette UK company. All rights reserved. "NIV" is a registered trademark of Biblica UK trademark number 1448790. Scripture quotations marked "ESV" taken from The ESV® Bible (The Holy Bible, English Standard Version®), copyright © 2001 by Crossway. Used by permission. All rights reserved. Scripture quotations marked "The Message" taken from THE MESSAGE, copyright © 1993, 1994, 1995, 1996, 2000, 2001, 2002. Used by permission of NavPress Publishing Group. Scripture quotations marked "J. B. Phillips" taken from J. B. Phillips, "The New Testament in Modern English", 1962 edition, published by HarperCollins. Scripture quotations marked "NLT" taken from the Holy Bible, New Living Translation, copyright © 1996, 2004. Used by permission of Tyndale House Publishers, Inc., Carol Stream, Illinois 60188. All rights reserved.
Extract pp. 108–109 *Just Like Jesus* © Max Lucado 2013, Thomas Nelson Inc. Nashville. All rights reserved. Reprinted by permission.
Extract p. 116 © 2009 Brennan Manning. *The Furious Longing of God* is published by David C Cook. All rights reserved.
Extract p. 142 *Under the Rainbow* © Catherine Campbell 2013. Published by Monarch Books.
Extract p. 155 *God's Empowering Spirit* © Gordon Fee 2009. Used by permission of Baker Publishing.

A catalogue record for this book is available from the British Library

Printed and bound in Great Britain by Clays Ltd, St Ives plc

This book is dedicated to Isabel Beattie, Ken and Peggy Wise, and Harry and Sally Henderson. You have each taught me the power of faith, the beauty of perseverance, and a love of truth.

For the Gold Hill Family — may the next chapter be the most exciting of our lives.

In loving memory of Fred Beattie, Frank Fadipe, John Clark, and all those whom the Lord has called home this year at Gold Hill. We miss them deeply.

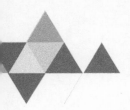

Contents

Conclusion

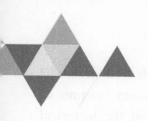

Foreword

When I was a young Christian, newly converted to the faith, there were many books being written to help believers explain their faith to others. They tended to major on the reliability of the Christian faith in historic terms: Did Jesus really rise from the dead? How can we be sure that Jesus Christ existed? Is there any truth in the miracle stories in the Gospels? Good scholars produced very readable and well-argued books to help us have confidence in the Good News of Jesus Christ.

There was also quite a lot of teaching and preaching to help Christians who weren't sure of their standing to have assurance that the Jesus they had put their faith in was to be trusted. Sometimes the image of Christ they portrayed was akin to that of an Edwardian English gentleman, whose word was His bond and who would go to any length to guarantee you salvation. He was eminently trustworthy and He'd said He wouldn't let go of you.

Now, I still believe that both those things are true: the story of Jesus – His life, death and resurrection, and the record of them in the Bible – is historical, true and believable; and God's word in Jesus Christ to His followers that He will never let go of us and that our life in Christ is eternally secure is to be trusted. But our current culture asks the questions differently – and wants different kinds of answers.

Is anything about a supernatural faith credible at all? Or are Christians, as secular humanists claim, victims of a self-inflicted God delusion? Never mind the historical stuff or the trustworthiness of God's word, what are you Christians on about when you claim that the world is charged with the grandeur of God? Why should faith be given a platform in today's public arena when it's clearly only the whim and opinion of a minority who cling to dead dogma and superstition? And what gives you the right to share your beliefs and the ethics you derive from them at work when I find the conclusions you draw totally offensive? Those are the hard questions of today – and there are few Christians who haven't faced those hard questions and their implications. Sometimes it feels as if Matthew Arnold's famous words in his poem "Dover Beach" have come to be our present-day reality:

> The Sea of Faith
> Was once, too, at the full, and round earth's shore
> Lay like the folds of a bright girdle furled.
> But now I only hear
> Its melancholy, long, withdrawing roar,
> Retreating, to the breath
> Of the night-wind, down the vast edges drear
> And naked shingles of the world.

Malcolm Duncan is a pastor, teacher, friend and co-conspirator in the Spring Harvest Planning Group. *Unbelievable* goes right to the heart of those big questions that now dominate the lives of Christians who are seeking to be faithful followers of Jesus Christ and witnesses to Him in today's world. This book is a conversation about this world and our place in it. It doesn't dodge the hard questions. It's brutally honest about the way it feels to have doubts. It takes us back to the story of God and what it means to inhabit that story. Malcolm reintroduces us to the Creed, not as an arid confession of faith, but as a living statement of our confidence in the God who has revealed Himself in Jesus Christ and lives in and through His Church in the power of the Spirit. God invites us to relationship – and in cultivating that relationship we rediscover confidence, re-affirm our belief, and reconnect to the mission of God.

Journey with Malcolm through the pages of this book – use it as a resource for discussion and study – and find again God's confidence in us and our confidence in Him. It's not so unbelievable after all.

Pete Broadbent
Bishop of Willesden and member of the Spring Harvest Planning Group

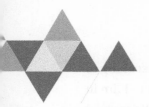

Acknowledgments

I cannot begin to express my gratitude to the Monarch team for their patience with me in this project. You have shown understanding beyond my wildest dreams. Thank you for absorbing the challenges I faced when my daughter was ill, which pushed the deadline for the manuscript back. As always, I consider myself blessed to be in partnership with you. I particularly want to thank Tony Collins, Jenny Ward, Simon Cox, and Andrew Hodder-Williams. I look forward to the years that lie ahead deeply humbled by your belief in me as a writer and as a communicator.

I also want to thank the Spring Harvest team. It's been a helter-skelter of a year and I am grateful to you all for your partnership. I am particularly grateful to Pete Broadbent for providing the foreword for this book. You all do a great job, and I pray God will continue to bless and encourage us as we journey forward. My prayer is that the best years are ahead.

The team at Gold Hill are fantastic and I am grateful to them. The whole church family is a joy, and I would not want to be anywhere else. Thank you for your love and prayers and for your support of my wider ministry. Without you, it wouldn't happen. Particular thanks to my eldership, Church Council, and staff team for the many times you have held me up in prayer. Particular thanks to Maria Bond, James Simmons, and Joyce Gledhill for your encouragement and support.

Thanks to my accountability group and to my friends

who pray for me and stand with me: John and Gill Newman, Duncan and Gill Stott, Brian and Isabel McCarthy, Terry and Jean O'Regan, and Christopher and Rachel Bird. Thank you.

My family deserve my deep thanks too. In a time of real illness and challenge, you have continued to support me and believe in me. You are *unbelievable!* Thank you to Debbie, Matthew, Benjamin, Anna, and Riodhna.

Lastly, my deepest and profoundest thanks and my worship belong to God. Without Him, there is just nothing to say.

Any truths you discover in these pages are the product of many minds and countless conversations. Any errors or omissions are, as always, my responsibility alone.

Section One

You become what you think

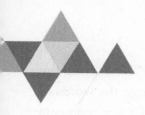

Chapter One

Lord, I believe; forgive my unbelief: The power of honest faith in a sceptical world

"I do believe, but help me overcome my unbelief!"

The words of a desperate father to Jesus
Mark 9:24

I believe in Christianity as I believe that the sun has risen: not only because I see it, but because by it I see everything else.

The words of C. S. Lewis, who described himself as the most reluctant convert in all of England

Is theology poetry?

The small chapel of rest was still and quiet. My father's remains lay before me, peaceful and lifeless. It was too early for the traffic on the Belfast street outside to be ramping up, so there was little noise to distract me.

My dad was dressed in his best grey suit, with his hair brushed and his hands folded across his chest. He was gone, and I was devastated. In a few hours, I would stand before the gathered mourners and conduct his funeral – the hardest thing I have ever had to do in my life. I'd wear two hats. The more important to me was that I was a son, his son. For the purposes of the funeral and the mourners, I was also the pastor, the "man of the cloth" conducting the service and guiding the congregation through the words of farewell and committal. I'd come to spend a few moments in quiet and to strengthen myself – and to say goodbye to him. I was confused, heartbroken, and bereft, but I knew I needed to do this. I loved him.

Why had God let this happen? No chance to say goodbye. No chance to hold his hand. No opportunity to thank him one last time for providing for me. No assurance that he had discovered God's love for him and made peace with his Creator. No assurance that I would see him again. The one single prayer I had consistently prayed lay in ashes before me – colourless and lifeless. I had asked God every single day for sixteen years to bring my father to a personal place of repentance and faith in Jesus. I had dreamt about serving him Communion. I was convinced it would happen – yet here I was about to conduct his funeral and I had no idea whether God had answered that prayer or not. Nothing to hold on to. Nothing to assure me of my dad's destiny. Just a dead body and a commitment to "do him proud".

So I wept over his body. I held on to the side of his coffin and I sobbed. Alone, with no one watching but God, I let my heart break. My tears fell on his corpse. My hands shook. My head ached and the questions began to erupt from my heart like a round of artillery fire at God. *Why did You let him die? Why did You do this? Why didn't You answer me? Why didn't You do something to help? What are You going to do now? What do You want from me? Where are You? Don't You care?*

The bullets just kept firing. Bang! Bang! Bang! Bang!

Then it subsided. I ran out of ammunition. I had no bullets left to fire, so I stopped. The sobbing continued but the purpose changed. Now I was sobbing and saying to God, *I can't take another step without You. I can't get through this day without You. I need You more than I have ever needed You and I feel You less than I ever have.*

The contradiction was stark. One minute I was shouting at God and wondering where He was, and the next I was telling Him I could not get through the day without Him. How does that make sense? I guess it doesn't, to many people. Either you believe or you don't. Either you trust God or you don't. But I don't really see it that way. I both trust God *and* struggle with Him. I believe in Him and I wonder where He is. The two things sometimes exist side by side in my head and heart.

As they placed the lid on my father's coffin, I stood like a sentry beside them. I still remember the sound of the turning clasps as they locked the lid to the coffin. Locking away my daddy. Locking away any last chance. It seemed like the sound of hope being locked away.

I turned and walked out in front of his remains. Outside were my darling mum, my three older brothers, and my older sister, Anne. None of them were Christians. Through the course of the day each of them helped me. My eldest brother literally held me up at the graveside when I struggled with the words, "Earth to earth, ashes to ashes, dust to dust, in sure and certain hope…". I didn't struggle with the first words, but with the last. Sure and certain hope?

Sure?

Certain?

Hope?

Hundreds of other mourners gathered, and the funeral went well. They said things like, *Good job! You did well! Your daddy would have been proud of you, so he would! I don't know how you did it, Malcolm! God bless you, son; thank you so much.* Of course I was grateful for the love and the support, but I don't think any of them knew how much I was struggling to keep it together and at the same time how utterly reliant I was on God to help me.

It was a struggle that would continue for months and months and months. Eventually I discovered a way through. I realized that I didn't have to understand God to trust Him. That helped me. It hasn't taken away my questions and it hasn't answered all my struggles; I have just realized that I can be honest about my questions. I don't have all the answers, and I don't care whether people think that makes me a good Christian or a bad one. I'd rather be honest than false. I am not going to pretend I understand God when I don't. I don't need to be perfect; I need to be authentic. It's only as I struggle that I grow.

I struggle with my faith.

That's OK.

There are times when the idea of "God" doesn't make any sense to me at all. I have questions that haven't been answered and some of the answers I *have* discovered are less than comforting to me. Some are about me, some are about the world, and some are about other people.

Why did God not stop the Boxing Day tsunami of 2004 that devastated so many lives?

Why (at the time of writing) is Robert Mugabe still in power?

Why does faith sometimes not make sense?

Don't misunderstand me – I can give you a theological answer. I can talk about the impact of sin and the power of choice, and the ultimate promise that God will put all things right. I can explain that evil is prevalent in the world, that we all have a natural propensity to selfishness and greed. I can answer the question with the same rigour as many others. I believe all those answers with all my heart – but I still struggle with God sometimes.

As a pastor, I find myself asking God why I have had to bury so many people whose whole lives were snatched away from them when they had barely begun. I get confused about that. I feel helpless trying to support mums and dads and sons and daughters who are mourning. I don't have the answers so I just weep with them, walk with them, love them. I'll gently point them to Scripture, help them say whatever they need to say to God, and suggest some of the biblical, spiritual, and pastoral things that will help them through this time, but I still do not always get God.

As a preacher, I ask myself how I can make a text that spans thousands of years and many different genres and addresses hundreds of different cultures make any sense whatsoever to the people I engage with today. There are bits that seem to fit well and others that don't seem to make sense or help at all. I don't always get God.

21

As a son, I wonder why my father died so suddenly in 2002 and why I never got the chance to say goodbye. As a father, I wonder why my son has had to struggle with illness for so many years. As a husband, I've watched my wife bravely battle illness and setback after setback and wanted to shout at God, "Enough already!" As a man, I've battled my own demons, faced my own illnesses, and struggled with my own doubts, weaknesses, and failures. I don't always get God.

Is it just me?

I don't think I am on my own in my struggles with my faith. I think millions of Christians struggle with God. I'd go as far as to suggest that if your faith is ever going to be real and lasting and genuine then you are going to have struggles. You'll face your own crises and fears. You'll have your own dark moments. I think we often want God to be God in ways that are not the ways of God at all. We want Him to make us feel indestructible instead of learning to trust that He is invincible. We want Him to remove pain from our lives instead of allowing Him to teach us, in the words of the old Welsh hymn, that *faith can sing through days of sorrow; all will be well.* I think we struggle with the God who is there because we want Him to be a different kind of God. We want Him to be a panacea and we'd rather reinterpret Him than reorientate ourselves. We'd prefer a nicer God, a safer God. We'd like to make Him more like us, because then people might like Him more. We think that because pain is present,

God must not be. The reality is, however, that God is not absent from the pain of the world; He is present in it. Listen to the words of Deena Metzger:

> God is the most fragile, a bare smear of pollen, that scatter of yellow dust from the tree that tumbled over in the storm of my grief and planted itself again. God is the death agony in the frog that cannot find water in the time of the drought we created. God is the scream of the rabbit caught in the fires we set. God is the One whose eyes never close and who hears everything.
>
> Deena Metzger, *Ruin and Beauty*

We forget that it is in the midst of our flesh-and-blood life that we meet God. He never comes in a vacuum. He always speaks *into* history from eternity and therefore we meet Him in the *reality* of life. It is in the midst of the messiness, the sadness, the pain, the joy, and the celebration and in *actual living* that we meet Him. We can *do* all things through Christ who strengthens us, Paul said to the Philippians. Paul did not suggest we could avoid the hard bits of life or its questions and uncertainties; he said we could face them.

Christian faith is not a highly developed avoidance technique

We Christians can end up thinking that "belief" and "doubt" are at opposite ends of the spectrum. It's easy to think that because we have questions, we cannot be "good"

Christians. That's a false dichotomy. The story of the man who wanted his son to be healed by Jesus, recorded in Mark 9, helps us to understand that:

> When they came to the disciples, they saw a great crowd around them, and some scribes arguing with them. When the whole crowd saw him, they were immediately overcome with awe, and they ran forward to greet him. He asked them, "What are you arguing about with them?" Someone from the crowd answered him, "Teacher, I brought you my son; he has a spirit that makes him unable to speak; and whenever it seizes him, it dashes him down; and he foams and grinds his teeth and becomes rigid; and I asked your disciples to cast it out, but they could not do so." He answered them, "You faithless generation, how much longer must I be among you? How much longer must I put up with you? Bring him to me." And they brought the boy to him. When the spirit saw him, immediately it threw the boy into convulsions, and he fell on the ground and rolled about, foaming at the mouth. Jesus asked the father, "How long has this been happening to him?" And he said, "From childhood. It has often cast him into the fire and into the water, to destroy him; but if you are able to do anything, have pity on us and help us." Jesus said to him, "If you are able! – All things can be done for the one who believes." Immediately the father of the

child cried out, "I believe; help my unbelief!" When Jesus saw that a crowd came running together, he rebuked the unclean spirit, saying to it, "You spirit that keep this boy from speaking and hearing, I command you, come out of him, and never enter him again!" After crying out and convulsing him terribly, it came out, and the boy was like a corpse, so that most of them said, "He is dead." But Jesus took him by the hand and lifted him up, and he was able to stand. When he had entered the house, his disciples asked him privately, "Why could we not cast it out?" He said to them, "This kind can come out only through prayer."

Mark 9:14–29

The words of this desperate father hint at where the real dichotomy lies in Christian living when it comes to faith. In verse 23, the father cries out to Jesus, "If you are able to do anything, have pity on us." Jesus' reply to the man is that all things can be done for the person who believes. At this stage, the man cries out to Jesus, "Lord, I believe; help my unbelief." He doesn't put "faith" and "doubt" as the opposites that are creating tension in his life. He puts "belief" and "unbelief" at opposite ends of the spectrum. It is as if he is saying, "I am believing as much as I can – I come as honestly and openly as I can; I am giving You *both* my belief in You and my unbelief in You, so do something with the belief I have and deal with the unbelief that I have." That is a very different thing from saying that his doubts somehow stop God from moving or lessen God's power. Perhaps if we come before God with honesty, vulnerability, and transparency, we offer Him a space in which to move and work. Perhaps He can do more with our authenticity than He can with our perceived "strength" of faith.

Like the father in this story and like me, many of us struggle with belief and doubt. We live in an age of deep scepticism and questioning in which we want reasons and explanations for everything. For many decades now, from perhaps as early as the beginning of the seventeenth century and the birth of the Enlightenment, reason and logic and rationality have been trying to push concepts such as "faith", "trust", and "truth" into the shadows. We have fallen into an intellectual elitism that suggests that if we cannot understand something, then we should not trust it. This increasing desire for "certainty" and "verifiable" answers is not at all wrong, but it can lead to a wrong place. It can lead to an over-defensiveness on the part of Christians and an over-dismissiveness on the part of non-Christians.

I wonder where we get the idea that Christians have to be certain about everything. Isn't it acceptable to say, "I am not sure"? Does God demand of us that we have absolute certainty about everything? I think not. I think we are allowed to ask questions. We are allowed to be honest. We are allowed to be authentic. Over the years of my Christian faith, I have discovered that I have less faith than I thought. I once thought my faith was like a mountain and the challenges it faced were like mustard seeds. I now think I have faith like a mustard seed and that the challenges I face are like mountains. At the same time, I have been heartened by the reality that Jesus told His followers that if they had faith as small as a mustard seed they could tell a mountain to move (Matthew 17:20).

I think I now have less certainty but more faith. I no longer feel the need to answer all the questions people put to me; instead, I know that there are a few deeply important questions that I must be able to answer and that my faith shapes my convictions about these things – and this somehow enables me to let go of the constant need to have answers. Let me give you a few examples.

If I am asked how God made the world, I can give you some suggestions, but I don't really know. Yet I am utterly convinced that He did.

If I am asked why God allows suffering, I'll point out some general principles that I think help, but I can't really answer the question very satisfactorily. Yet I am utterly convinced that God understands our suffering as a participant and not as a bystander.

If I am asked why evil exists in the world, I have some basic responses that might further the discussion but I can't really give you a full defence. Yet I can tell you that I believe that God is good and His love endures for ever.

If I am asked how the cross of Jesus works, I can give you broad answers that are rooted in the Bible and the traditions of the Church, but to be honest it is still a deep mystery to me. Yet I know it works because I have experienced its transforming power in my life.

To bring it full circle, if you ask me why God let my

dad die I can't give you an answer, but I can now say that I trust God and one day He will answer that question when I ask Him. Ironically, on the day He does so, I don't think the answer will matter very much at all. In the meantime, I am learning to trust God, and I don't need to have all the answers and be able to explain everything in order to trust Him. I may not know much about Him, but I know He is a loving Creator, who made the world and has a plan and a purpose for it and for me.

Theology is much more like poetry than it is mathematical formulae, journalistic prose, or legal defence. While our statements about God should be accurate, descriptive, and clear, they should also allow room for mystery, wonder, and worship. There is much we know about God, but this pales into insignificance compared to that which we do not know. We must allow ourselves to enter the mystery without the need to completely understand him. We cannot entirely contain the uncontainable. We cannot completely explain the inexplicable. To have faith means to trust, and we can trust God without having to completely understand Him. This is true in any relationship – we do not have to completely understand someone to trust them.

The power of honest faith in a sceptical world

Trust and faith are out of fashion. Think about all the great institutions and symbols of trust, confidence, and authority in our nation, and how we respond to them, and we will see the level to which our "trust" and "faith" have been eroded. Trust and confidence aren't at a particularly high level either when it comes to what we believe or how we live out our faith.

External challenges

Broadcasting agencies and the media have had their reliability questioned because of scandals concerning abusive partners, phone tapping, self-serving board members, and journalistic deceit. Police authorities have been undermined by the way they have handled football tragedies, cover-ups, and the deliberate smearing of people in the public eye. Politicians are perceived as selfish, untruthful, and morally suspect because of their handling of expenses and their constant inability to give a direct answer to a direct question. Bankers and financial institutions have suffered a deep loss of credibility because of fixed lending rates, over-borrowing, and self-preservation. Food supplies are suspect because of the use of dubious sources and supply chains. Schools and universities have been guilty of changing league tables. Hospitals and social care facilities have treated patients badly and neglected those who are the most vulnerable. It's not a particularly "trust-inspiring" picture, is it?

Challenges to the Church

"The Church" is tarnished by revelation after revelation of abusive priests, covered-up investigations or failure to provide a moral lead for society on a wide range of topics.

Internally, we have major discussions on a number of issues from sexual ethics to the importance and role of men and women in the Church, not to mention heated discussions on how we make decisions and what the priorities of the Church should be in the twenty-first century. If we are not careful, we argue over the secondary matters while the world around us struggles to discover its meaning and purpose. We eagerly debate sexual ethics but ignore the challenge of the boardroom. Many local Churches seem to be poorly led, with preaching that doesn't relate particularly well to our daily lives or modern society. Petty church politics can eat away at our credibility. Services, structures, and budgets in local congregations can all too often reflect the needs, desires, and preferences of those who are already part of the church family, and ignore the needs of those outside. That isn't a particularly "trust-inspiring" picture either, is it?

We need a way of being confident in a sceptical world

Our society is asking big questions, and we often look as if we are fumbling about in the dark for answers. Questions such as:

- How can Christ be the only way in a world of religious diversity?
- Why do Christians seem to think they have a right to a place in public life?
- Does Christian education strengthen or weaken those it seeks to teach?
- What is marriage?

- How can the Church refuse to bless gay relationships?
- How can you expect us to take the Church seriously if you ignore women in your structures and leadership models?
- Why should we take the Church or Christianity seriously at all?

Many of these questions are being asked not only by those outside the Church but also by those within the Christian community. There are, of course, many answers to the questions that we face. The Church in the United Kingdom, as elsewhere, has some brilliant leaders, preachers, teachers, and apologists. We have men and women who are positively and enthusiastically engaging in the issues of our day and seeking to shape public opinion and lead discussion rather than always being on the back foot. There are robust, sensible, engaging answers to ALL the questions I have set out above if we only take the time to listen to the arguments.

Yet it strikes me that there is *still* a lack of confidence in the Church in the United Kingdom and North America. We don't just see it in the big questions that we listen to on the radio or watch on the television or engage with through other media. We see a lack of confidence in the way we explain our faith to our friends and family. We see it in our fear of sharing the story of our own relationship with God. We often see it in a basic inability to explain what *being a Christian* actually means. We are losing the ability to articulate our faith, to share our story, to engage in dialogue, and to point people to Jesus.

The need for confidence

As a matter of urgency, we need to discover how to strengthen our confidence in the purposes and plans of God. If we do not find a way of doing that, we run the risk of creating an increasingly weaker Church, in all the wrong senses of the word. Not weak as in servant-hearted, or weak as in poor. I do not mean weak as in free from political power and on the margins of society, or weak as in claiming no God-given right to tell people what to do. For many of us, including me, this kind of weakness would be most welcome! No, I mean weak as in disconnected from our purpose and our roots or weak as in lacking any authentic encounter with God Himself. I mean weak as in failing to develop robust, strong, and holistic disciples who understand everything they are and everything they do to be a reflection of what they believe about God, His purposes, and our place in His world. If we do not do something to discover confidence again, we will pass on the baton of a shallower Gospel, we will stand in the shadow of a smaller cross, and we will raise up leaders with a diminished and curtailed vision for the world than God would have them pursue. The weakness I fear most is not a weakness created by what other people say or do to us. Instead, the weakness I fear most is that of a Church that has lost its moorings, drifts into the fog of relativism, and scuppers itself on the dangerous rocks of popularity and acceptance.

Martyn Lloyd-Jones, who was once the pastor of Westminster Chapel in central London, argued that when the Church is absolutely different from the world, she invariably attracts it. He suggested that it is when we are distinct as Christians that the society around us wants to listen to us, even if society hates us for a while first. Francis Schaeffer levelled this great charge against the Evangelical Church, naming it the "great evangelical disaster":

> Here is the great evangelical disaster. It is the failure of the evangelical world to stand for truth as truth. There is only one word for this, namely, accommodation. The evangelical church has accommodated itself to the world spirit of the age.
>
> Francis Schaeffer

Answers that connect to people

My experience tells me that we need answers that connect, both for ourselves and as we reach out to others. They need to make sense. Most people don't want big, sweeping academic solutions to their questions, although we *must* maintain *intellectual* rigour as we address the big issues that we face. But first of all our answers must be grounded. They must be real. They must actually help people to understand what it means to be a Christian and what it does not mean. Just like the man who wanted Jesus to heal his son, most Christians today say to Jesus, "I do believe, but help me overcome my unbelief." We want ways of connecting with God that are reliable. We want a better understanding of God and a better experience of Him. We want answers that connect with our work, our homes, and our families.

We want a framework that will stand the test of time. We want a strong foundation. We want a way of understanding

God, the world, and our place in it that will continually enable us to be faithful to Christ and effective for Christ. We need the energy to keep going and we want a clear sense of purpose and direction. We want confidence in God and we need to know that God has confidence in us.

Such a framework of faith is not only possible, it already exists.

- The foundation is the truth of God as revealed to us through the Bible.
- Our way of understanding God, the world, and our place in it is found in the great credal statements of the Church.
- The energy we need is found first in conversion and then in being continually strengthened and empowered by the Holy Spirit.
- The clear sense of purpose that we need is found in God's purposes for His Son as lived out through the Church, His bride on earth.

Our confidence is in God who has revealed Himself to us through His Son, Jesus, and has made plain His plans and purposes in the unchanging Gospel of Christ, and it is to this that we now turn. C. S. Lewis, writing in 1945, said:

> I believe in Christianity as I believe that the sun has risen: not only because I see it, but because by it I see everything else.

We need a similarly God-centred vision of ourselves, our world, and God's beautiful purposes for it. It is to such a vision that we now turn.

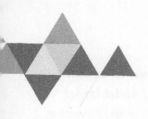

Chapter Two

Anchored, not drowning: The truth of the Gospel in a changing world

It's news I'm most proud to proclaim, this extraordinary Message of God's powerful plan to rescue everyone who trusts him, starting with Jews and then right on to everyone else! God's way of putting people right shows up in the acts of faith, confirming what Scripture has said all along: "The person in right standing before God by trusting him really lives."

Paul to the followers of Christ in Rome
Romans 1:16 (*The Message*)

Among men it is customary to swear by something greater than themselves. And if a statement is confirmed by an oath, that is the end of all quibbling. So in this matter, God, wishing to show beyond doubt that his plan was unchangeable, confirmed it with an oath. So that by two utterly immutable things, the word of God and the oath of God, who cannot lie, we who are refugees from this dying world might have a source of strength, and might grasp the hope that he holds out to us. This hope we hold as the utterly reliable anchor for our souls, fixed in the very certainty of God himself in Heaven, where Jesus has

already entered on our behalf, having become, as we have seen, "High Priest for ever after the order of Melchizedek".
The writer of the book of Hebrews to early Jewish followers of Jesus across the world
Hebrews 6:16–20 (*J. B. Phillips New Testament*)

I believe I have heard God's voice speaking clearly and unequivocally to me twice. The first time was when I was converted to Christianity. The simple words "Son, come home" changed my life. Even as I write, I remember those three words and they instil hope in my heart that this journey of faith I have been on since 1986 is right and good and true.

The second and only other time I have (so far) heard God clearly was when our second son was born. It was 1997 and we were at the Elim Bible College in Nantwich, Cheshire. Within just eight weeks of Benjamin being born, he became extremely ill and we were told that he was going to die. I remember going home from the hospital to phone family and leaving Debbie with our little boy. I was devastated. How was I going to tell the family this terrible news? I drove back to the flat where we were living and parked the car. I walked to the flat, my mind a blur and my heart broken.

Once inside, I remember falling to my knees and weeping. I do not know how long I wept for or even what I said, but I prayed as I have rarely prayed. For however long I was on the floor in the hall, I just called out to God. Then I heard Him. Two simple words as if spoken by Someone right beside me. The *same voice* that I had heard eleven years before, leading to my conversion, now spoke to me again. He said, "He's mine." Immediately a deep peace descended on my heart and I have never lost it. God did not tell me that Benjamin would get better. He did not tell me that Benjamin would die. He just told me that Benjamin was His. I have never doubted it since.

Those words have held me through many ups and downs with our boy. We celebrated his eighteenth birthday at the end of 2013 and he is still going strong, but what holds us, and what holds him, above all other things is the conviction that God spoke.

Those words have been like a deeply rooted and immovable anchor for Benjamin and for us all. No matter what has happened, no matter how many times he has been ill or faced uncertainty, we have known the assurance of God's strong words. Even when I have questioned God about His purposes for Benjamin and why He has let my son carry the burden that he has had to carry, I have simultaneously been held by the anchoring promise of His word.

Truth that holds us like an anchor

When everything around us is changing, we need something that will anchor us and hold us firm. Christianity has such an anchor – it is the Gospel of Jesus Christ as given to us in the Bible. It is not dependent on the most recent fashion, social trend, or theory. This message of "Good News" holds us firm in whatever storms we face as individual followers of Jesus and as part of His body, the Church, on earth. There are a great many discussions about what "the Gospel" is.

Some would argue that the "Gospel" is that we should repent because the Kingdom of God is at hand:

> Now after John was arrested, Jesus came into Galilee, proclaiming the gospel of God, and saying, "The time is fulfilled, and the kingdom of God is at hand; repent and believe in the gospel."
>
> Mark 1:14–15 (ESV)

Others would argue that the Gospel can be summed up by the phrase "Jesus is Lord":

> If you confess with your lips that Jesus is Lord and believe in your heart that God raised him from the dead, you will be saved.
>
> Romans 10:9

> ...and every tongue confess that Jesus Christ is Lord, to the glory of God the Father.
>
> Philippians 2:11 (NIV)

Others would argue that the Gospel is summed up in the idea that Jesus died for our sins and that as we believe in Him we are rescued:

> For God so loved the world that he gave his only Son, so that everyone who believes in him may not perish but have eternal life. Indeed, God did not send the Son into the world to condemn the world, but in order that the world might be saved through him.

Those who believe in him are not condemned; but
those who do not believe are condemned already,
because they have not believed in the name of the
only Son of God.

John 3:16–18

Still others would point to the summary of the ministry of
Jesus that is found in Paul's first letter to his young protégé,
Timothy, the pastor of the Church in Ephesus:

Without any doubt, the mystery of our religion
is great: He was revealed in flesh, vindicated in
spirit, seen by angels, proclaimed among Gentiles,
believed in throughout the world, taken up in glory.

1 Timothy 3:16

All these verses seem to me to indicate the beating heart
of the Gospel that resonates through all Jesus is and all he
does: that He came to proclaim the Kingdom of God and
call people into it; that He has been established as Lord
over all and that to enter His Kingdom you must follow
His instructions and submit to His will and purposes and
turn from your own way; that His is a central message of
hope, love, and forgiveness, which is made possible by
His own sacrifice and driven by the Father's love for us,
and that Jesus, in Himself, was God in flesh and bone,
was affirmed and approved by the Holy Spirit, was seen
by all the powers of all the ages as the true King, has been
preached to the Gentiles and the Jews; that all who believe

in Him are transformed by His grace and power and that He now stands, physically and spiritually alive, in glory. Yet there is another description of the life and ministry of Jesus that, I think, conveys to us the central and core tenets of the Gospel. It is found in Paul's first letter to the Corinthians:

> Now I should remind you, brothers and sisters, of the good news that I proclaimed to you, which you in turn received, in which also you stand, through which also you are being saved, if you hold firmly to the message that I proclaimed to you – unless you have come to believe in vain.
>
> For I handed on to you as of first importance what I in turn had received: that Christ died for our sins in accordance with the scriptures, and that he was buried, and that he was raised on the third day in accordance with the scriptures, and that he appeared to Cephas, then to the twelve. Then he appeared to more than five hundred brothers and sisters at one time, most of whom are still alive, though some have died. Then he appeared to James, then to all the apostles. Last of all, as to one untimely born, he appeared also to me. For I am the least of the apostles, unfit to be called an apostle, because I persecuted the church of God. But by the grace of God I am what I am, and his grace toward me has not been in vain. On the contrary, I worked harder than any of them – though it was not I, but

the grace of God that is with me. Whether then it was I or they, so we proclaim and so you have come to believe.

1 Corinthians 15:1-11

The importance of these words

Paul introduces this section of his letter to the Corinthians by telling them that he wants to *remind* them of the Good News. In verses 1 and 2 he wants them to understand that this is the message that has changed their lives. It is this message that will continue to hold them and save them as they *continue* to believe in it and live it out.

He then goes on to use language that is rarely seen in his letters. Once or twice in other places, such as when he speaks of the Lord's Supper (1 Corinthians 11), he uses the phrase "for I handed on to you... what I in turn had received". There is a sense of passing on a baton here. The words and the content of the message that Paul is about to repeat to the Corinthians are not something that he has dreamt up himself. He has not made it up. He is *passing it on*. Not only that, but he is *passing it on* just as *he has received it*. You get the impression that this is about a truth or a set of truths that have been given to Paul and which he is now giving to the Corinthians.

Some would describe all this as the *apostolic Gospel*. It is a succinct, clear summary of what Paul understood to be at the heart of the message of the Lord Jesus. I agree with that. Scott McKnight, in his excellent book *The King Jesus Gospel*, and Tom Wright, in his equally compelling book *How God Became King,* point to the evidence of the establishment of the lordship of Jesus in the resurrection and the establishment of Jesus' Kingdom as the central assertion of the Gospel in this passage. That has to be a central truth of the Good News, I think. Jesus did not simply come to die. He came to live. His whole life and ministry establishes His Kingdom and advances the cause and the purpose of God. The reality of the King and His Kingdom has to sit at the heart of the Good News of the Christian faith.

The Good News of the Kingdom liberates us from the tyranny of any other "lordship" that seeks to dominate, control or own us. Because Jesus is King, Caesar is not. That reality would mean that many of the early Christians were dispatched to ruthless and traumatic martyrdoms. The kingship of Jesus meant that Herod could not be king. It means that the Greek philosophers could not be king. It means that reason could not be king. Nothing else can be king when Jesus is King.

First importance?

But look again at the passage I have quoted and you will discover that there is more than simply the "Kingdom" being presented here. The other aspects of this "handed-down" or "apostolic" Gospel are not just add-ons to the main statement of the resurrection. Together they form the very fabric of that which we must hold on to because these truths actually hold on to us. Read 1 Corinthians 15:1–11 very slowly and you will discover that there are constituent parts that make up this "anchor" Gospel that holds us steady and keeps us safe:

- Christ died for our sins (verse 3)
- Christ was buried (verse 4)
- Christ was raised from the dead (verse 4)
- Christ proved His resurrection by appearing to the Apostles (verses 5 and 7)
- Christ proved His ongoing life and power by appearing to over 500 witnesses at once (verse 6)
- Christ proved His ongoing ministry and power by also appearing to Paul himself and calling and equipping Paul to be an Apostle (verses 8–11)
- All of this was done *in accordance with the scriptures* (verses 3 and 4).

Paul's language makes it clear that all these constituent parts of the message he proclaimed were *both* "Good News" *and* of "first importance". Together these parts form an anchor that keeps us steady in the midst of great change. Together they enable us to continue in our faith and in our witness. These truths together stop our ships from sinking.

There is too much of a rush to make the "Kingdom" the only thing that matters here or in the rest of the New Testament. The Kingdom of God lies at the heart of the great purposes of God, but how could that be established without a sinless and perfect life such as Christ's? How could sin and death, the great enemies of the Kingdom of God, be defeated without the atoning and substitutionary death of Christ *"for our sins"*? How could this victory be proved without clear

43

evidence for the *resurrection*? And how could any of this make sense unless it was done *according to the Scriptures*? I think Christ's death can make sense only because of His life, and His resurrection can make sense only because of His death *and* life. His resurrection, death, and life, however, can make sense only because of His *purpose*, and all of it makes sense only because of the *Scriptures*.

I find that summary remarkable and inspiring. It is remarkable because it is, relatively, so very brief. It is inspiring because it is so simple. The Good News of Jesus is all about... Jesus! Who He was and who He is. What He did and what He does. The Good News can be seen only in Him and He can be encountered only in His authentic self, purpose, and mission according to the Gospels (the word actually means "good news"), and they cannot be fully understood without the background of the Scriptures.

So the anchor that holds us is the anchor of the whole of Jesus' life and death and resurrection *according to the Scriptures*. In other words, the Bible and its description of Jesus' person, purpose, and power sits at the heart of any understanding of Jesus in our lives and our cultures today. This is of *first importance*.

We can't change Jesus

Paul warned the Corinthians that they could not change Jesus. He told them that it was only as they held on to the message of Jesus as revealed in the Scriptures that they could continue authentically to live out His life and His purpose.

What was true for them is also true for us. We can't

change Jesus to fit our culture any more than we can change the principles of life. Yet so often we try to! Some would argue that we should take the "bits" of Jesus that we don't like or can't quite relate to and ditch them so that we can make Him more popular. Bits like the virgin birth, for example. Surely that isn't important? Or perhaps His humanity? Or perhaps His deity? Or perhaps His dying for our sins? Or perhaps His resurrection? Or maybe His appearances to His disciples and the apostles? Or maybe His miracles? There are those who would argue that, if the story of Jesus found in the Old and the New Testament is a bit hard to accept, we should just change the story. Forget the details of His messiahship. Forget He was a Jew. Forget He suffered and died. Forget the idea that He gave His life as a ransom for many. Just make Him popular and approachable.

Why doesn't Paul do that, then? Why doesn't Paul make Jesus fit into Corinthian culture? Why doesn't he tweak his core message to make Jesus more palatable? Well, frankly, because he cannot. He is not permitted to. Paul doesn't understand the Gospel as *changeable* at all. It must be handed on *intact*. He makes similar arguments in his letters to the Galatians, to the Colossians, and to the Philippians. He refuses to compromise on the Gospel – he even calls it "His Gospel".

Paul did not envisage a culturally bound Jesus. To him, to speak of the Kingdom without understanding its Jewish and scriptural basis would not have made sense. To make Jesus subject to our culture either lightens the anchor or weakens the rope that ties us to it. If we lighten the anchor, then we create a Jesus who is not strong enough to keep us steady when the pressures and challenges of our world press in on us. A light anchor will just get dragged along the seabed and the ship will hit the rocks. If we weaken the rope that ties us to the anchor, then we will become disconnected from the source and we'll end up shipwrecked.

Lightening the anchor

Jesus is unchanging. He is the only way to a full relationship with God. His is the only name given to people by which they can truly know what God is like. Other religions and spiritual practices may take us some of the way towards seeing and knowing God, but only Jesus takes us to the very heart of God. Paul made it clear in his letter to the Colossians that to see Jesus is to see God. To encounter Jesus is to encounter God. Jesus Himself told His disciples that when they had seen Him, they had seen His Father. We can't make Jesus more palatable. This throws up some very important questions for us, I think.

Why did Jesus never apologize for His Father? Why did He live so faithfully as a Jew? Why did He overturn the teaching of the Pharisees and the Sadducees and those who tried to make God look like what they wanted Him to be? Why did He focus on the ideas of repentance, holiness, change, obedience, and sacrifice and not offer a "live how you like" approach? Why did He talk about heaven and hell and truths and consequences so much? Why did He quote the books of the Hebrew Scriptures so often? Why did His first followers and then the Early Church look to the truths and the power of the Hebrew Scriptures to understand themselves? Why were they willing to die rather than deny some of the challenging and disconcerting claims of Christ? Why did the New Testament Church root itself in the Hebrew Scriptures?

I think the reason is that they understood that they could not change the Gospel. I also think they knew that if they tried to make Jesus more popular or make Him fit into their culture, they would run the risk of causing people to have confidence in the wrong thing. What good is high confidence in thin ice?

In his letter to the Romans, Paul emphasized that the Gospel he believed in still had the power to change lives. This Gospel, he argues, is still the power of God for salvation to those who believe. We must be careful to listen to the words of the New Testament and we must be even more careful not to dismiss Paul. His confidence in the Gospel should propel us to a similar confidence. We are fooling ourselves if we think we can make the Gospel any stronger by changing it and we are in even greater danger of delusion if we think we can make Jesus more effective by making Him more "relevant". There is a vast difference between popularity and power. A Jesus who never challenges us, does not confront us with our sin, and never asks us to change is always going to be more popular, but when we hit the rocks of our culture, our conscience or our hidden lives, we will wish that we had not made the anchor so light.

Our confidence doesn't lie in the hope that the storm will pass. Our confidence lies in the reality that the anchor holds, no matter how strong the wind.

We are not free to change Jesus.

Weakening the rope

What is the rope that ties us to Jesus? If we cannot change *Him*, can we change the rope that ties us to Him? In a sense, of course we can. We can weaken the connection to the Jesus of historical Christianity as much as we want. The test will come when the storm hits. Will the rope that ties us to the anchor hold us or snap?

In many ways I think this image of being "tied" to Christ lies at the heart of this book. Around us rage the storms of scepticism. Inside and outside the Church there is an attempt to separate from the uncomfortable and perhaps even slightly naïve pictures of Jesus. A gruesome punishment and death are so old-fashioned! The concept of God pouring out His wrath on His Son is so out of keeping with our ideas of parenting and fatherliness. A God who asks us to be sexually faithful doesn't understand the challenges of the twenty-first century, does He? All this talk of self-sacrifice, faithfulness, laying down your life, giving up all you have for the sake of the Kingdom of God. It is simply a metaphor for fitting Jesus into the rest of your life, right? Wrong.

As I write, we are in the Advent season. That is a time of the year when we reflect on the preparations for and the true meaning of the Incarnation. We remind ourselves of Who it was Who came to earth to save us. We contemplate our own Christian lives and we think about our own weaknesses and failures. We remind ourselves of the hope that springs from the reality that Christ came once as a baby and will come again as the reigning King. We allow space and time for Him to work in us, to confront us, to cleanse us, and to prepare us. We don't make Jesus fit our plans; He asks us to fit into His.

I am reminded of Jesus' calling of Nathanael, recorded in John 1. When Nathanael is invited to follow Jesus, he comments on the fact that Jesus comes from the undesirable town of Nazareth. He asks, "Can anything good come from Nazareth?" The implication is clear – you don't expect me to trust in someone as common and low as a man from Nazareth, do you? The answer of course is that the disciples do. Nathanael is changed by his encounter with Jesus, and we can be too.

Yet the world around us still scoffs at Jesus and His Church. You don't want to tether me to something as simplistic, as puerile, as childish as the idea of a God who came to live on earth, died on a cross, was buried, and then rose from the dead, do you? You can't seriously expect me to take literally the stories of raising the dead, walking on water, feeding 5,000 men with a handful of bread and fish? You're not really willing to stake your life on a bunch of old letters and books written by misogynists and uneducated peasants, are you? Are you actually suggesting that the stories of a God who punished people in the Old Testament and asked a man called Abraham to be willing to sacrifice his son are part of your story? How ridiculous! You cannot be asking me to believe that nonsense? Actually, yes, I am.

"What does the Bible mean?" versus "What does the Bible mean to me?"

I want to suggest that one way of looking at the rope that ties us to the anchor is to think of it as the link that ties us to the God who is at work in Jesus.

There has been an interesting shift in the dynamics of Christian theology, I think, which is beginning to have an even deeper impact on our spiritual lives and our churches. Many Christians have replaced the fundamentally important question of "What does the Bible mean?" with the more personal question, "What does the Bible mean *to me*?" By doing so we have, without realizing it, subjectivized the Gospel and made it into a consumer product.

Paul's whole approach to the matter of sharing the Good News of Jesus was to be faithful to the story of Christ – but to use language that the people around him understood and could relate to. If we fail in this attempt at contextualization for both ourselves and our culture, then we fail to connect Jesus to the world. John Stott called this the art of "double listening" and he believed that all preachers should be expert in it. I agree. We simply cannot treat the Bible as if it will automatically make perfect sense to anyone who listens to it being explained or reads it for themselves. We must seek to understand the Bible in its original context before we can try to explain it in our own. We must not, however, change its original meaning. To do so is to cut the rope. In order to understand "what the Bible means to me" we must first seek to understand "what the Bible means".

This is the hardest and most challenging duty of a pastor or a preacher: to wrestle with the text of the Bible and to discover, as closely as we can, what it meant when it was first heard. Only as we seek to do that can we then apply it to our context and our culture. When we forget the original context of the Bible, we are believing in nothing more than a new and improved version of the society we like or belong to. However, when we forget the context into which we must apply the truth, we end up sounding out of touch, out of step, and out of sorts! God's truth is never mediated into a vacuum from a vacuum. It is never "timeless" in that sense. It is spoken *into* a culture. We simply must wrestle with what it meant before we can explain what it means.

When we make "what the Bible means to me" more important than "what the Bible means", I can really understand what we are doing and why we are doing it. My concern is not simply that such an exercise is unhelpful; it is that such an exercise cuts you and me off from the truth of the "faith once delivered". The Christ of the Bible is the Christ that we have – we are not free to create Another.

Who shapes what? Does the Bible shape our culture or will our culture shape the Bible?

I love the fact that Christianity is engaged in the world. Thank God that this faith we hold calls us to be "in the world but not of the world". We are not called to stand on the edge of the game and shout at everyone else. We are called to be in the game, on the field, involved in the story. We must be careful, however, not to become so enmeshed in the culture that we lose our ability to critique it.

It strikes me that the great question at the heart of all questions for twenty-first-century Christians everywhere is what we will do with the Bible. All other questions about our place in the world as Christians – how we live, the choices that we make, the values that we hold, the principles and ethical choices that shape us – all these can be changed to reflect our preferences if we make the simple choice to make the Bible, as a foundation, less important than our culture.

It is my conviction that many Christians are losing sight of the centrality of the Bible in shaping our understanding of Jesus, His mission, and His call upon us as His disciples. If we are not careful, we will end up with a Church that is popular, but spiritually powerless. If we allow the culture around us to become the dominant voice in our heads and our hearts then we will be able to justify almost any moral conviction we want and endorse almost any decision that is required to keep us included and popular. It will be a poisoned chalice, though. Slowly, perhaps imperceptibly at first, we will look less and less like the disciples of Jesus and the early Christians. To be honest, I think this has already had quite a deep impact on the Church in North America and in the United Kingdom. I often think we are making discipleship more like gym membership than like a biblical pattern of living. Our preaching, teaching, and forms of Church so often seem more like a good concert, or, even worse, a nineteenth-century lecture. By allowing ourselves to be shaped by the culture, we have chained the Bible and its power to a particular generation or mindset. We have limited the revolutionary power of Jesus and we have missed the point.

Any half-decent student can *read* the Bible, but it is entirely different to let the Bible read you. The great challenge to our generation is whether we will allow the anchor of the Lord Jesus and His purposes and plans for the world, which perfectly reflect the purposes and plans of His Father and His Spirit, to shape us, or whether we will cut the rope and ride the sea. If we do the latter, it is my utter conviction that the witness of the Church in the United Kingdom and North America (for these are the areas where I minister most and hence the places on my mind and heart) will be shipwrecked. We will have nothing to say, and when we do, we will not be heard because we will have lost the ability to say it.

Wrestling with truth – learning to be tethered to the Gospel

Years ago I faced a dilemma as a Christian. I was struggling with huge parts of the Old Testament and much of the New. How could I believe in this angry God? What could I say to people who have problems with the blood-curdling, revenge-driven passages in the Old Testament or the apparent endorsement of slavery and male dominance in the New? Of course I realize that this position is a caricature, but the question is, I have no doubt, one you will understand. I came to the point at which I was ready to abandon the idea of the Bible being inspired and instead choose to believe that the bits of it I liked were inspired and the other parts could be, on the whole, relegated to "not helpful".

The simple revelation that Jesus did not apologize for His Father caused me to reconsider my position entirely. If Jesus accepted the Hebrew Scriptures and the images of His Father and did not feel a need to defend Him or give Him a facelift, why did I feel the need to try to redefine Him? After a great deal of prayer, reflection, and waiting on God I made a simple decision of faith. I would accept the Bible as God's inspired and infallible word as originally given. I would not stop fighting it, wrestling with the truth I found in it, throwing questions at the Holy Spirit, and seeking to use all of my limited intellectual and emotional abilities to wrestle with the text. I would not pretend that I understood the parts of it that I did not. I would always assume a position of submitted but determined humility in my engagement with the Bible. When my ethics conflicted with the Bible's, then mine would be deemed wrong, and when that decision itself seemed wrong, I would accept that this was because my whole world view was so affected by my sinfulness that I could not rightly determine what was morally good and morally bad. I would never make myself seem nicer, kinder or more accepting than God. Instead I would wrestle with the text as Jacob wrestled with God in Genesis 32. I would fight the text. I would engage with it. I would argue with it. I would dig into it. I would hammer it with the tools of biblical, linguistic, cultural, and social analysis. I would bring all my gifts and talents, whatever they were, to the task of understanding the Bible and trying to teach it to those God entrusted to my care. But the Bible, inspired and given by the Holy Spirit, would always win. I would also be defeated by the truth of God as revealed in Scripture. In short, I would learn to walk, like Jacob, with an increasing limp and that limp would become my posture and my hallmark as a Christian leader. Why? Because I would rather limp *under* the authority of God's word than march under the apparent liberty that the tyranny of my belief in my own superiority would bring.

This, to me, is the great challenge facing our generation of leaders and of Christians in general. We need a second reformation that cries, "Scripture alone!" once again. The first Reformation came about because people could not access the Bible and believed what they were told it said without having the tools and the resources to read it for themselves. Men and women, hungry to discover the truth, fought and died so that the Bible might be available and might be the tool that was used by God to shape and fashion His Church.

The reformation we need now, which I would suggest is the only pathway to a renewed confidence in God and a renewed sense of God's confidence in us, is one in which we once again return to the Scriptures. This time it is birthed out of the reality that people have such free and ready access to the Bible that they take it for granted. They still prefer other people to tell them what it means. They will accept doctrines, practices, and convictions based on the level of celebrity of the preacher or the author. That will not do. It is as dangerous as the context of the first Reformation. We need a new generation of men and women who will once again cry, "Scripture alone" but who this time will seek to help people pick up their Bible and let it shape their lives. We need a reformation that will see the quest for cultural relevance replaced with a deep passion for a radical transformation of our culture which is shaped and fashioned by the power of the Holy Spirit as He lifts us to the Jesus of Scripture who points us to God the Father as revealed in the Bible.

Will your anchor hold?

Recently I went to see a member of my congregation who was gravely ill. He and his wife had served the Lord faithfully during more sixty years of married life. Their names are Fred and Isobel Beattie, and I love them. This book is dedicated to them. Fred was promoted to Glory a few weeks later.

Fred was a Boys' Brigade captain for many years. He sought to help young boys and men meet and be changed by Christ. When I went to see him in hospital, I took an old hymn book with me and sang him the Boys' Brigade hymn. It was written by Priscilla Owens in 1882:

> Will your anchor hold in the storms of life,
> When the clouds unfold their wings of strife?
> When the strong tides lift, and the cables strain,
> Will your anchor drift or firm remain?

Anchored, not drowning

We have an anchor that keeps the soul
Steadfast and sure while the billows roll,
Fastened to the Rock which cannot move,
Grounded firm and deep in the Savior's love.

It is safely moored, 'twill the storm withstand,
For 'tis well secured by the Savior's hand;
And the cables, passed from His heart to mine,
Can defy that blast, thro' strength divine.

It will surely hold in the Straits of Fear –
When the breakers have told that the reef
   is near;
Though the tempest rave and the wild winds
   blow,
Not an angry wave shall our bark o'erflow.

It will firmly hold in the Floods of Death –
When the waters cold chill our latest breath,
On the rising tide it can never fail,
While our hopes abide within the Veil.

When our eyes behold through the gath'ring
   night
The city of gold, our harbor bright,
We shall anchor fast by the heav'nly shore
With the storms all past forevermore.

I held his hand as I sang it, and tears rolled down his face.
When I had finished, he gasped at me and with what little

breath he had, he said, "My anchor holds, Malcolm! My anchor holds!" There was a gentleman on the other side of the ward who was also a patient and when I turned to look at him, he was crying too. I asked him how he was and he said to me, "I stopped believing in God sixty years ago. I convinced myself He wasn't there. I've just changed my mind."

You see, there is a longing to be connected to this Anchor deep within the human heart. The Anchor always holds. We cannot understand the Anchor that is Jesus without ourselves being anchored in the Scriptures that point to Him.

We must remain anchored to the Bible, tied to it by bonds of faith and faithfulness. We must learn how to speak into the culture instead of just mirroring it. When we do this, we will rediscover a fresh and powerful confidence that God may not be finished with us yet. But we must do so without sounding arrogant, triumphalistic or prideful. So how do we do that?

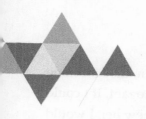

Chapter Three

Confident, not arrogant: The impact of hope in a despairing world

Now who will harm you if you are eager to do what is good? But even if you do suffer for doing what is right, you are blessed. Do not fear what they fear, and do not be intimidated, but in your hearts sanctify Christ as Lord. Always be ready to make your defence to anyone who demands from you an account of the hope that is in you; yet do it with gentleness and reverence. Keep your conscience clear, so that, when you are maligned, those who abuse you for your good conduct in Christ may be put to shame. For it is better to suffer for doing good, if suffering should be God's will, than to suffer for doing evil.

Peter's guidance to early Christians
1 Peter 3:13–17

The problem is not that Christians are conservative or liberal, but that some are so confident that their position is God's position that they become dismissive and intolerant toward others and divisive forces in our national life.

John Danforth, US Ambassador to the United Nations,
Faith and Politics (2006)

If I ever get the chance to meet Angela again, the first thing I will do is apologize to her for being so arrogant. If I could have the chance to replay the time that I knew her, I would do it. I not only put her off Church, I put her off Jesus.

I'd been living in Falkirk, Scotland, for a few years and had become part of a new church plant there. In fact, I had moved to Falkirk from Dundee, where I had been studying, so that I could get more involved in the life and ministry of the Church. Angela lived in the flat below me and she was not a Christian. I was desperate to see her come to faith in Christ, and pretty determined to "help" her understand how much she needed to experience the grace of God. After months and months of being asked, she eventually came along to one of our services. Afterwards, I sat with her for almost two hours, repeatedly urging her to make a "decision" to follow Christ. I was forceful, rude, and bullish. Every question she asked I answered with arrogance, although at the time I thought I was just being confident. I wore her down. I led her in a "prayer of salvation" and she left. I was delighted with myself. I convinced myself that God had drawn her into a relationship with Himself.

She never came back to Church and she never spoke to me again. When she saw me, she'd go in the opposite direction. She avoided me at all costs. Why? Because I was a bully. I tried to coerce her into Christianity. I bombarded her with the Bible. I was arrogant, prideful, and wrong.

It took me a while to realize what I had done. At first I just told myself that Angela was struggling to let go of her old life, that she was going through the birth pangs of new faith. Of course that wasn't true at all. The poor woman was just fed up with me. I often pray for her now, and ask God to undo my stupidity. I have peace that God has forgiven me, but I do wish I had the chance to put it right. If, by some miracle, you are reading this and you know Angela – or maybe you *are* Angela – I am really sorry. Don't let people who behave like I did put you off Jesus.

Arrogance – an off-putting characteristic

One of the most off-putting witnesses to the wider world is an arrogant, vitriolic, and angry Christian. You know the kind of person I am describing, don't you? I am talking about people who have an answer for everything, the sort of people who shout at you instead of listening to you. I became a Christian in Northern Ireland and I have to confess that most of the people around me in my early days as a Christian were loving, gracious, and kind. They gently helped me to see who Christ was and they supported me in my new-found faith. Not all of them were like that, though. One of the central reasons for my not becoming a Christian earlier had been the attitudes and the behaviour of one or two very well-known Christian leaders in Northern Ireland who were also involved in politics. These people were always angry. They were always asserting their position with such forceful certainty. When you listened to them, they were constantly cutting others down, dismissing opposite points of view. They were so quick to make judgments and so good at pointing the finger, and they always seemed to think they were right. I wonder how many people in Northern Ireland have been put off Christianity by such a witness.

We hear a lot about aggressive secularists and atheists, but we hear less about aggressive Christians. Yet it strikes me that an aggressive Christian is a contradiction in terms. You don't see Jesus doing a lot of finger wagging, but, when you do, He is normally addressing religious leaders who are asserting their own position and trying to control others. I think there is a great danger for the Church, and I have to say particularly for the Evangelical Church, that we have become known for what we stand against rather than what we stand *for*. By and large, people associate us with a list of negatives. They can tell you what we don't believe and what we don't like. They have more difficulty in telling you what we stand for. That is because we have assumed that we are being confident when we are actually being arrogant.

I've always believed that the *way* we speak is just as important as *what* we say. I remember watching a film some years ago in which one of the characters said, "Be careful what you say 'Amen!' to, because somewhere a child is listening." I've watched people say the right thing in the wrong way and as a result they have pummelled and beaten another human being with their words. It's ugly. I've also watched people say the *wrong* thing in a gracious and loving way with the opposite results. Although their arguments were weak, their attitude was beautiful, and as a result, those listening gave them the benefit of the doubt.

There is no clearer area where there is a need to think

about the difference between "confidence" and "arrogance" than that of human sexuality and marriage.

I hold a conservative and traditional view on human sexuality and marriage. That is to say, I believe the Bible's teaching is very clear on these matters, namely that God has ordained marriage as a covenant relationship between a man and a woman and not between two people of the same gender, and that sexual intimacy is a gift to be explored and enjoyed within the confines of marriage and is never right outside that context. I realize that my view is often perceived as being in the minority and that many would view my position as old-fashioned. I cannot do anything about that, but it doesn't make me feel I need to change my view. The UK is undergoing a massive change of attitude in these areas and the government has been pushing through legislation to enable same-sex marriage. That has caused a great deal of debate, discussion, and campaigning.

One of the organizations that has arranged lobbying and campaigning on this issue is the Coalition for Marriage. They have been seeking to support the traditional, orthodox view of the issue and to challenge the government to think about the way it has handled the debate. I have to say that I have been very impressed by the gracious but firm and clear way in which the Coalition has conducted its campaign. They have not been arrogant or angry, but they have been clear. There have been other Christian voices, however, that have been quite offensive in the way they have engaged in the debate. They've attached labels to people and shown real intolerance. It's been quite embarrassing sometimes to listen to or watch those who claim to be "Christian" in their views yet have behaved in such an unChristlike way. We need to be careful how we speak; the world is listening.

People are looking for confidence, but they are put off by arrogance

Most people are attracted by confidence, but repelled by arrogance. There is an attractive quality about people who have assurance and confidence and combine that with humility and gentleness. They somehow make you feel at ease. When you are in the company of a confident person, you are able to be yourself, to ask questions, and to engage in discussion. You don't feel threatened by them; instead, you feel drawn to them. You may not always agree with them, but at least you respect them.

When I think about the people in my life who have been confident, I think of teachers who knew their subject, such as Eamonn Foster and Mr Piddington. These two men combined great knowledge and depth with great openness. They *encouraged* me by their confidence. When they answered my questions, they did so in a way that drew me into greater learning. The lecturers who had the most impact on me were those who combined the traits of confidence and humility. People such as Siegfried Schatzmann, who taught me Greek and the New Testament, Peter Davies, who taught me the Old Testament, Julian Ward, who taught me systematic theology, or Keith Warrington, who taught me the Gospels. These men were confident but not arrogant.

They drew me in.

When I think of people who have put me off a particular subject, they have often been those who were arrogant. Leaders who never allowed for the possibility that they might be wrong. Preachers who spoke as if they alone were right and seemed to exhibit a hermeneutic of pride and presumption rather than humility and openness. I'd much rather listen to a politician, for example, who has a clear view of what they think is right but is able to exhibit a level of humility and to dialogue with others than to one who shouts other people down, wouldn't you? Maybe if we had more politicians who were willing to dialogue and listen we'd have a stronger public life.

People like confidence. They like to know where you stand, to hear what you think. What they don't like is your telling them where they must stand or what they must think. It's one thing to present people with your views and your ideas as graciously as you can and then recognize that they are free to make a decision and to live with its consequences. It is quite another to try to force people to accept your view and to endorse you. People are open to persuasion but they are most definitely closed to coercion. That is as it should be, because we are called, as Christians, to try to persuade others, but we are never called to coerce them.

So what is the difference between confidence and arrogance, and how can we grow in confidence without sounding triumphalistic and arrogant?

The difference between confidence and arrogance

Everybody knows someone who sings their own praises at work, or places themselves in the middle of the room at every social opportunity. You may sometimes wonder if they know something about self-confidence that you don't. Perhaps their annoying habit is a sign that they've discovered some secret to waking up every day feeling ready to conquer the world. Truly, the line between confidence and arrogance can seem finer than it really is. Arrogance springs fundamentally from a wrong view of yourself. That wrong view will be for one of two reasons. Either you are masking low self-esteem with cocky overcompensation, or you have too high a view of yourself and think you are always right.

Confidence springs from assurance, and arrogance springs from pride. Confident people have a realistic view of their own traits and abilities and trust themselves enough to respond to life authentically. They learn from failure rather than letting it define them, and they are always open to learning. They believe that there is something to be learnt from others. Arrogant people don't have an honest view of themselves. They either undervalue or overvalue their own abilities. They tend not to learn from failure and they would rather run away from authentic dialogue than engage in it.

Having confidence is wonderful and a positive quality with which to navigate life successfully. It allows us to overcome fears and doubts and to take control of life's decisions. Confident people are easy to be around. Others typically view a confident person as dependable and admirable. However, as is often true, too much of a good thing can become a bad thing. Overconfidence leads to arrogance, and arrogance is off-putting.

1. Confidence doesn't always have to be right, but arrogance does

Confidence is not a belief that one is always right or a sense of being unable to fail. True confidence welcomes alternative perspectives and opinions. A confident person will rarely be found lecturing or preaching to others on how they are wrong. Believing you are always right and being unable to accept influence from others can make you obnoxious to be with. Confidence means being willing to be wrong and knowing you'll be OK if you are. Confidence enables us to show vulnerability and admit to past mistakes.

2. Confidence enables you to affirm others; arrogance doesn't

Both the confident and the arrogant person will be aware of personal areas of strength and ability. However, a confident person has little difficulty in seeing others' gifts and strengths, while the arrogant cannot. Additionally, a confident person does not insist on being adored by others for their skills or abilities. People who are confident do not use words as weapons. There is a quiet calm in the truly confident that the arrogant do not possess. If you find yourself constantly trying to impress friends, family or others with your skills and abilities, you have crossed the line into arrogance.

3. Confidence is rooted in security; arrogance is rooted in insecurity

Confidence and arrogance come from different sources. Confidence springs from security. A confident person can accept their weaknesses or faults with grace – even though they may not like them. Arrogance is rooted in insecurity – a defence from feelings of weakness that are unacceptable and unclaimed. An arrogant person generally has a skewed view of the world and a warped understanding of themselves.

4. Confidence avoids comparisons; arrogance feeds on them

Arrogant people build themselves up by putting others down – to "win". Arrogant people feel good about themselves through affirming their superiority to others. Genuinely confident people feel great about themselves without comparing themselves with others. Arrogant people tend to bluff their way to success and often have difficulty listening to others. Arrogance leads to overcaution and to blaming others or circumstances if things do not work out as expected.

5. Confidence is robust; arrogance is fragile

Arrogant people can and often do have successes, but there are significant costs. Relationships are often shallow and superficial or strained, and can also be fragile owing to difficulties in accepting guidance and feedback and an impaired ability to accept and learn from mistakes.

Arrogant or confident faith?

When we combine these traits we end up with two broad descriptions. An arrogant assertion of Christian faith will be one that always has to be right, finds it hard to affirm the views of others, is rooted in fear and insecurity, constantly compares itself with others, and finds it hard to face criticism for fear of failure or losing the argument. A confident assertion of Christian faith, on the other hand, doesn't always have to be right and is able to accept that it is sometimes wrong and is open to and welcoming of other people's points of view without feeling the need to endorse or reject them immediately. It is rooted in a deep sense of security and acceptance and does not compare itself with others in order to gain validation. A confident assertion of faith is open to criticism and flourishes in authentic settings and contexts.

Confidence and hope

A confident articulation of Christian faith leads to hope. People around us do not want to hear cocky answers and arrogant assertions. They don't want to be told what to believe or how to behave. They reject Churches and Christians who coerce or dictate to them. So they should. You do not see such traits in the life and ministry of the Lord Jesus, for example. Did He ever force anyone to do anything? Isn't one of the core aspects of God's relationship with His Creation that He fundamentally lets us have our own way but also tells us that in having our own way we must accept that we live with the consequences of our decisions and actions?

I'm told that people are not interested in God any more. I am not so sure. I think they are not interested in religion very much. I think they reject a presentation of Christian faith that denies them the chance to think, question, reflect, or discuss. Perhaps that is why approaches such as Alpha and Christianity Explored work so well for so many – they create space for dialogue and discussion. People are just as hungry for hope as they have ever been, but they want a hope that makes sense. I wonder if one of the great challenges for us as Christians is that we are not confident of our faith and what it means, and therefore we are apprehensive and unsure about how to share it.

In order to share the hope of the Gospel with others, we ourselves need to know what that hope is, and in order to know what that hope is, we must know what we believe. Do we know what we believe? Are we confident in our faith? Are we anchored? Are we afraid of our own doubts?

What sits at the heart of our faith?

In order to be confident about our faith before others, we must discover again what our faith means. We need to discover the grace of God again.

God is far kinder than we could ever dream of. He is far more beautiful. He is far more gracious. He is far more forgiving. He is far more willing to accept us as we are and to change us than we are willing to accept Him as He is. He loved us before we ever knew Him (Romans 5:8) and His commitment to us is far stronger than our commitment to Him (1 John 4:19). He has dealt with the sin that separated us from Him and restored us to a right relationship with Himself (1 Peter 2:24). He has given us gifts so that we can serve Him (1 Corinthians 12) and He has committed Himself to producing His character in us (Galatians 5:22–23). He is committed to using the Church to show His purpose and beauty in the world (Ephesians 3:10) and to shining through us as we serve Him (Matthew 5:13–16; Ephesians 2:10). He has promised to finish the work He has started in us (Philippians 1:6), and He is fundamentally committed to the transformation of the whole planet (Habakkuk 2:14). The Good News is good news for every person at every level. God is better than we could ever imagine!

For many people, the idea of this kind of God is just unbelievable. The concept of a loving, forgiving, and self-sacrificing God is just too good to be true. We live in a culture that says that there is no such thing as a free lunch. This is too good to be true: we definitely don't deserve this kind of God. In a society that believes you don't get anything for nothing we just can't understand the lavishness of God. There *must* be a catch in the Gospel, mustn't there? There has to be a secret clause somewhere, surely. Becoming a Christian must be a contract in which the small print says that God will love me only if I clean up my act first and sort myself out, right? Wrong.

Most Christians find it difficult to believe the Gospel in its entirety. In an attempt to make God more manageable, we domesticate His grace. We put far more conditions on His acceptance of us than He does. Over the years we accommodate our notions of having to earn God's love or having to do something to make sure that He *still* loves us. As a result, we begin to believe things that are clearly not true about Him. For example, we think that we can separate ourselves from God, that there are some places we can go where God does not go – yet God Himself makes it clear that He will never leave us (Deuteronomy 31:6; Hebrews 13:5). There is nowhere that we can go where He is not present.

If we are not careful we end up distorting the Gospel because we are unable to cope with the sheer goodness of it. In distorting the Gospel, we distort God Himself. For example, those of us who come from a "Protestant Evangelical" tradition can fall into the terrible trap of having come to faith because we have discovered the grace of God but living our Christian life on the hamster-wheel of trying to please Him. On the other hand, those of us who come from a Roman Catholic tradition can end up picturing God as an angry old man who delights in punishing His Creation and who can never be pleased. Those of us who find our home in the charismatic traditions of the Church can end up believing in a God who is with us only if we "feel" Him. The truth is that we can all end up making God look like a pale version of who He really is if we are not careful. In the words of Brian McLaren:

> Accumulating orthodoxy makes it harder, year by year, to be a Christian than it was in Jesus' day.
>
> Brian McLaren, *A Generous Orthodoxy*

What do we really believe?

Michael Novak is an American, a philosopher, and a Roman Catholic. In his book *Belief & Unbelief: A Philosophy of Self-Knowledge* he identifies three ways in which we "believe" and hold our conviction.

Public belief

This is what we want other people to think we believe, though we do not believe it. We may have a hidden agenda or some anxiety about what people would think of us if they knew what we really believed. Whatever the reason, we want people to think we believe something when we actually do not believe it at all.

An example of "public belief" is the story of King Herod, who pretended to want to know where the baby Jesus was so that he could worship Him, when the truth was that Herod actually wanted to kill Jesus.

Private belief

This is what we actually *think* we believe, but we do not believe it because, though we claim to believe it, and genuinely think we do, we do not live it.

An example of this could be the story of King David and his adultery with Bathsheba. David genuinely believed that he was seeking to honour Yahweh, but his lifestyle and his beliefs contradicted one another.

Core belief

Core belief is what we really believe. It is not seen in what we say; it is seen in what we do. Our words flow out of our convictions, and our convictions shape our actions.

An example of this is the teaching of James in his epistle, when he speaks of how we treat the poor. He says that faith, without the accompanying demonstration of our convictions, is worthless.

Margaret Thatcher became known as "The Iron Lady" because of her tough approach to politics. A film of her life was given that title and released in 2011. In the movie she is portrayed as a conviction-based politician. She remains one of the most divisive characters in British politics. You either loved her or hated her, but the one thing you could not do is be unclear about who she was or what she stood for.

In *The Iron Lady*, there is a scene in which Margaret Thatcher goes to see her doctor. He asks her how she is feeling, and her riposte is swift:

> People don't think any more, they feel. "How are you feeling?" "Oh, I don't feel comfortable"; "Oh, I'm so sorry, we, the group, we're feeling…" Do you know, one of the great problems of our age is that we are governed by people who care more about feelings than they do about thoughts and ideas. Now, thoughts and ideas, they interest me… Watch your thoughts, for they become words. Watch your words, for they become actions. Watch your actions,

for they become habits. Watch your habits, for they become your character. Watch your character, for it becomes your destiny.

Margaret Thatcher in The Iron Lady

We become what we believe

What I truly believe about God is not simply what I say. It is not what I recite. What I truly believe about God is seen in how I live. It is seen in the way that I treat people, what I do with my money, how I handle those with whom I disagree. It is reflected in what I give my time, my energy, and my attention to. Too often, we allow ourselves to be lulled into the idea that if we say something, we believe it. That just isn't true. The truth is that if we believe something, then we will *live* it, and in order to reinforce what we *believe* we must *live it out,* even when we do not feel like it.

As uncomfortable as it might be, our Churches, our Christian communities, reflect what we actually *believe* about God. They demonstrate our priorities, our values, and our convictions. If we want to know what we believe about God, then we need to look at the way we behave and the way our *Churches* behave.

That might prove a little uncomfortable for many of us, but it is an important principle. Yet, at the same time, we all know the struggle and the pain, and perhaps the personal dilemma, of actually doing things we don't want to do! Like the apostle Paul (Romans 6 and 7), we find ourselves absolutely committed to something in our heads, hearts, and intentions, but not always following it through in our decisions, attitudes, and actions. It would appear that we can, sometimes, believe something yet at the same time seem not to believe it. There are lots of reasons for this apparent paradox.

We've a lot to be confident about

> Though an army encamp against me,
> My heart shall not fear;
> Though war rise up against me,
> yet I will be confident.
>
> Psalm 27:3

In the midst of all the uncertainties of life and the unpredictability of events around us, we can be confident that God is good and that His love endures for ever. We don't have to pretend to have all the answers; we can be honest about our questions, open about our struggles, and humble enough to admit our own faults and failings. God is strong enough to cope with our uncertainties. He doesn't expect us to be perfect; He expects us to be honest.

In the next section, we explore a set of core convictions that have sat at the heart of Christian faith for almost 2,000 years. They unite us, strengthen us, and guide us. When we understand the truths behind them, we have something profound and powerful to say to the world around us. They root us in the Gospel that has been delivered to us. They give us confidence to share who God is and what God does with a world that is desperately in need of hope. They are called the Apostles' Creed.

76

Section Two

Discovering
the power of
confidence in
God

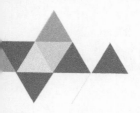

Chapter Four

The Apostles' Creed: Unbelievable faith in a sceptical world

I BELIEVE *in God, the Father Almighty,*
creator of heaven and earth.
I believe in Jesus Christ, his only Son, our Lord.
He was conceived by the power of the Holy Spirit
and born of the Virgin Mary.
He suffered under Pontius Pilate,
was crucified, died, and was buried.
He descended to the dead.
On the third day he rose again.
He ascended into heaven,
and is seated at the right hand of the Father.
He will come again to judge the living and the dead.
I believe in the Holy Spirit,
the holy catholic Church,
the communion of saints,
the forgiveness of sins,
the resurrection of the body,
and the life everlasting.
Amen.

The Apostles' Creed, based on the Old Roman Creed (c. AD 100)
and dating from around the end of the fourth century AD

Why the Apostles' Creed?

Unbreakable... Unbelievable

Josh and Sophie, who were brother and sister, were once playing in their living room. They had built a tent and, as they crouched inside, they had invented their own little world. It was full of adventurers and pirates and heroes. To build the tent, they had secured one corner of a sheet on the mantelpiece by placing a heavy old ornament on top of it to act as a weight – but they were careful not to move the ornament in case it broke. They were always conscious of not wanting to break the ornament, but as the afternoon progressed they began to enjoy the game. At the same time, they began to forget about the ornament.

As they were swaying on the open sea and Josh was defending Sophie from the ferocious pirate who had just boarded the ship, Josh jumped up with his wooden sword. As he did, the sheet lifted high above his head. Josh and Sophie saw the ornament on the corner of the mantelpiece fly up into the air. They winced as they waited for the terrible noise of it hitting the hearth and breaking into tiny pieces. They knew they were going to be in so much trouble! Instead of breaking, however, the ornament bounced along the hearth and came to a halt at the feet of their mum, who had just walked into the living room because she had heard the commotion. She bent down and picked up the ornament and looked at Josh and Sophie.

"Good job this is unbreakable!" she said, smiling. She placed the ornament back on the mantelpiece and told the children to be careful.

Josh looked at Sophie, his young eyes wide with wonder. "It's unbreakable, Sophie," he gasped. "If we'd known that in the first place, think of the fun we might have had!"

Unfathomable... Unbeatable... Unstoppable

Christian faith is unbreakable. It is not a porcelain figurine made to be handled fearfully and tentatively. It is indestructible. It is robust. It can face the challenges of our culture, the anxieties of our heart, and the questions of our sorrows and doubts. This faith changes us. It transforms and renews us because at its centre there is a Father who is unfathomable, a Son who is unbeatable, and a Spirit who is unstoppable.

In this section I want to try to help us to see this God again, to rejoice in who He is and what He wants to do in the world through us and what He wants to do in us.

God has not finished with you yet. He hasn't finished with His Church yet, and He hasn't finished with the world yet. The best is yet to be.

Unbelievable.

A Creed that unites us

If you are a follower of Jesus Christ then you are one of around 2 billion Christians in the world today. That's just under one-third of the world's population. There were around 1,600 Christian streams and denominations in the world in the year 1900. Today there are somewhere between

21,000 and 34,000! There are, however, just five major blocks of Christian belief today. These are (listed alphabetically):

- Roman Catholics (around 1 billion people)
- Orthodox (around 218 million people)
- Anglicans (some of whom would be happy to be described as Protestants and others would not) (around 70.5 million people)
- Independents (around 275.5 million people)
- Other Protestants (around 400 million people).

There are many things that divide us. From the rite of baptism to the way we celebrate the meal that remembers the death of Jesus and how we handle the Bible, there are a lot of different views and conflicting ideas. We have varying views on the roles of priests and pastors, the different roles of men and women, the place and form of worship and music in the life of a Church, and the way in which we make decisions and govern ourselves. Many of these divisions are an embarrassment to the Church and a bad witness to the world, but some of them are helpful and good.

Yet every single major Christian denomination and stream in the world today is united in acceptance of the Apostles' Creed. This statement of belief and confession of what we, as Christians, hold to be central to our faith was first mentioned in a letter written by Ambrose, the Bishop of Milan, in AD 390. If you are from one of the more established traditions of Christianity, then you may well have been encouraged to learn it so that you could repeat it by heart. It is often used in Anglican and Roman Catholic Churches to prepare people for the rite of confirmation and, in most of the established Protestant traditions of Christianity, it is affirmed in early confessions and catechisms that were (and are) also used to help Christians in those traditions understand what they truly believe. Many of us may not know very much about the Apostles' Creed. We may even wonder why it is important to affirm it. What does it matter? Well, it matters for lots of reasons – here are just a few:

- The Apostles' Creed has united Christians for somewhere in the region of 1,620 years.
- It cuts through many of the "non-vital" issues and focuses on the heart of the matter.
- It affirms great truths that hold us in the midst of great controversies and challenges.
- It is thoroughly rooted in the books and letters of the New Testament and probably captures the teaching and convictions of the Early Church in a way that can be remembered.
- It is a "living confession" that is still used by the vast majority of Jesus' followers around the world.
- It is a statement of BELIEF and of FAITH: not just words that we recite, but truths that change us and shape us.
- The Apostles' Creed gives us confidence and reminds us that we are part of the wider Church around the world, not just one small Church on our own.
- It reminds us of the greatness of God and of what He has done to redeem and transform us and the world in which we live.

Understanding the Apostles' Creed

This section of *Unbelievable* is rooted in the Apostles' Creed. In each chapter, I will be exploring the Creed with the Trinity in mind: the Father, the Son, and the Holy Spirit. I want to explore some of the great biblical truths that lie behind the Creed and help us to see the ways in which confidence in what we believe can translate into confidence in how we live.

To help us understand the theology behind the Apostles' Creed, I want to look at it through the lenses of three core statements at the heart of it:

- I believe in God, the Father Almighty...
- I believe in Jesus Christ, His only Son, our Lord...
- I believe in the Holy Spirit...

By looking at this ancient credal confession, we will be rooting ourselves in the truths of Scripture about God and His purposes in the world. We'll discover again that God has a purpose and a plan for His people, His Church, and the world. As we stop and think about the great truths at the heart of Christian faith, we will discover that it is possible to face a world of uncertainty with confidence, and without sounding arrogant. As we focus on God, we'll find the attention shifting from us to Him. When that begins to happen, confidence begins to rise in us because we realize that God has not finished with us yet.

An unbelievable faith – the power of faith in a sceptical world

One of the great beauties of the Christian Church is our ability to adapt and be flexible. Christian communities meet under trees in Africa, hidden away in homes in the Middle East, in tin sheds in the townships of South Africa, and on boats in Cambodia. It is wonderful to see the way we are adapting and changing to be more connected to our communities here in the UK and in North America. We are learning how to "do" Church and "be" Church differently. We use pubs, clubs, schools, warehouses, and homes. We teach through preaching, discussion, and debate. We are adapting how we lead, the language we use, the songs we sing, and the metaphors we employ. It is wonderful. Our agenda has broadened to include matters that have always been on God's heart but sometimes not on ours: issues of environmental awareness, human freedom, the rights of children and women, eradicating poverty, unfair governments, and exploitation. I am sure that such diversity thrills the heart of God. We are releasing leaders, equipping the saints, and dreaming of what could be.

I am excited to be a church leader at this moment. As I write, the Church I lead has just made the massive decision to move away from the church building we own and seek to build a new community centre that will be a hub, a heart, and a home. We want to use our resources to bless our wider community, so we want to build a hub for community activity, a place that will be the heart of community life, and only thirdly will be a home for our church family. We want to build it to meet the needs of the wider community, not our own. We aren't the only Church that is aiming to serve others first and put ourselves last. Many across the world are doing it.

Yet there is an area in which we are not free to innovate and change and come up with new ideas. That is the area of what we actually believe. In a world full of scepticism and cynicism, it would be all too easy for Christian denominations to abandon the idea of the "faith once delivered" and come up with a contemporary faith that meets the "needs" of twenty-first-century people. People have attempted to do this in every generation. Get rid of the aspects of God that are unpopular, demythologize the Gospel, make Jesus more realistic and God more contemporary, and you will win the hearts of many. I have no problem at all in changing how we communicate the Good News of Jesus Christ, but I am deeply concerned at the thought of changing the Gospel itself.

That's where the Apostles' Creed comes in. This unique and powerful articulation of the faith that has held the Church together for 1,620 years is as potent and persuasive now as it has ever been. The people around us aren't seeking boxed-up little answers or a domesticated God; they are looking for an authentic encounter with God – and by extension, with people who know what God is like. We are not free to change this Gospel, but we can become familiar with it again.

At the heart of the Apostles' Creed we discover powerful,

world-changing articulations of who God is and how He has dealt with the world. These statements speak into the greatest needs of our society and the deepest longings of the human heart. They point to a God who is powerful yet personal, tangible and tender yet able to transform, intimately connected with the world, and deeply involved with sustaining, and, yes, redeeming the universe. We must not abandon the old ways, Jeremiah told the people of Israel. Preach the Gospel, Paul told young Timothy. Stand for the truth, Luther declared.

We stand at a moment in history when the sands of society are shifting quickly. It is too early to tell which of those sands will turn out to be death traps and which will turn out to be stable. The biblical and spiritual truth articulated in the Apostles' Creed, however, has stood the test of time. We must learn it again, and allow it to be absorbed into our heads and our hearts. We must let this powerful declaration of what the Church believes invade our thinking, captivate our imagination, and recreate our future. In its words lies the power to present a God who is strong enough to save and close enough to reach.

We can change many things but we cannot change the truth, and it is the Truth and only the Truth that will set people free. We need to embrace this faith once delivered and guard it. We need to stand up for it. We need to become captivated by it again. And, as we do, a sceptical world will once again take notice of a Church that actually believes that God is powerful, Jesus is Lord, and the Holy Spirit is active in the world.

Perhaps our generation is the one that has been given the privilege of defending the power of the Gospel to one another because the next generation will be the one that pushes into territory that we never thought we could reach. I want to help them to reach further than I can. I want to enable those Christians coming behind me to stand on my shoulders.

I want to pass on to them a confidence in the Gospel and a confidence in God – that He really is changing the world.

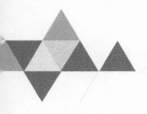

Chapter Five

Unfathomable:
I believe in God, the Father
Almighty...

I BELIEVE in God, the Father Almighty,
creator of heaven and earth.

For all who are led by the Spirit of God are children of
God. For you did not receive a spirit of slavery to fall
back into fear, but you have received a spirit of adoption.
When we cry, "Abba Father!" it is that very Spirit bearing
witness with our spirit that we are children of God, and
if children, then heirs, heirs of God and joint heirs with
Christ – if, in fact, we suffer with him so that we may also
be glorified with him.

The apostle Paul to Christians in Rome
Romans 8:14–17

When Israel was a child, I loved him,
*   and out of Egypt I called my son.*
The more I called them,
*   the more they went from me;*
they kept sacrificing to the Baals,
*   and offering incense to idols.*
Yet it was I who taught Ephraim to walk,
*   I took them up in my arms;*

but they did not know that I healed them.
I led them with cords of human kindness,
  with bands of love.
I was to them like those
  who lift infants to their cheeks.
  I bent down to them and fed them.

The prophet Hosea to the people of Israel
Hosea 11:1–4

By far the most important aspect of theology is "who God is". If we get this wrong, then everything we think about our faith will be skewed.

It is because I believe in God, the Father Almighty, the Creator of heaven and earth, that I know that I am loved. Without this core conviction at the heart of my faith, God would be a tyrant and I would hide from Him in fear. It is the concept of God as our "Father" that is so utterly transforming. The Reformer Martin Luther said he would spend eternity trying to understand just two words from the New Testament, "Our Father". It is this conviction that takes us beyond God as a distant ruler or an uninterested party and into the realms of intimacy, involvement, and hope.

Christianity doesn't believe that God is just an idea or a thing or an it. Embedded deep within the Christian tradition is the concept of God as a Someone who wants to be found. "Seek me and you will find me when you seek me with all your heart," wrote the prophet Jeremiah (Jeremiah 29:13). This invitation is worth taking up – it could change our lives.

A discovery worth making

"To fall in love with God is the greatest romance; to seek him the greatest adventure; to find him, the greatest human achievement," wrote Augustine of Hippo. C. S. Lewis said this:

> There are only two kinds of people in the end: those who say to God, "Thy will be done," and those to whom God says, in the end, "Thy will be done." All that are in Hell, choose it. Without that self-choice there could be no Hell. No soul that seriously and constantly desires joy will ever miss it. Those who seek find. To those who knock it is opened.
>
> C. S. Lewis, *The Great Divorce*

In his book *Standing for Something,* the writer Gordon Hinckley says:

> Let us never forget to pray. God lives. He is near. He is real. He is not only aware of us but cares for us. He is our Father. He is accessible to all who will seek Him.
>
> Gordon B. Hinckley, *Standing for Something: 10 Neglected Virtues that will Heal our Hearts and Homes*

There is no doubt that God yearns for a relationship with us. The question is whether we will search for Him. The writer of Psalm 103 exactly captures the yearning and searching heart of God:

As a father has compassion for his children,
so the Lord has compassion for those who
    fear him.
For he knows how we were made;
he remembers that we are dust.

Psalm 103:13–14

The idea of a God who longs for a relationship with us is almost unfathomable. Why would this be the case? Could it possibly be true that God has made us for Himself and that our hearts are restless until they find their rest in Him? It would appear that the earliest Christians believed this was so important that they embedded their convictions in the opening line of the Apostles' Creed:

I believe in God, the Father Almighty,
Creator of heaven and earth.

God at the centre of it all

Though the word "Trinity" is not used in Scripture, this word describes a doctrine found throughout the Bible – the truth that there is one God, who exists eternally in three persons: the Father, the Son and the Holy Spirit. We see these persons at work in Creation as the speaker, the word spoken and the breath that carries the commanded word. We see them in evidence at the baptism of Jesus and in His transfiguration. We see them at work on the cross as Jesus dies. We see them described in the last words of Jesus to His disciples, recorded in John's Gospel, chapters 14–17, and sometimes called the Farewell Discourse.

The Apostles' Creed opens with an affirmation of the Trinity – identifying one member of the Trinity as God the Father. This shows that God is relational – He has always existed within relationship within the Trinity. He is not dependent upon man for relationship, and yet He chooses to have a relationship with man. When we enter a covenant relationship with God we can know Him as our perfect Father. This means that we can know that we are completely loved, not because of what we have done, but because we are His.

The story of God as portrayed in the Bible is the story of a God who wants to reveal Himself to us. He is a God who tells us His story and invites us into it. He is not a distant God, but a God who describes Himself as our Father and it is because He is our Father we have an assurance that we are loved and wanted. I am aware that many struggle with the notion of God as a Father because of the difficulties they have faced in their relationships with their earthly fathers, and I address the challenge and the opportunity of this in the last section of the book. It is enough to say here that for those of us with such struggles (and in many ways I would count myself in that number) the image of God as a Father can act like a magnet that draws us towards Him rather than pushes us away. It is a question of allowing the polarity in our own lives to be changed, so that we can be drawn towards Him. From personal experience I can say that I have discovered God to be the father I longed for, the father I desperately needed. Discovering God as my Father enabled me to love my earthly father more deeply than I would ever have thought possible. God's fathering heart can bring healing and confidence in the deepest areas of our lives and our personalities.

If we grasp this single principle, it changes everything for us

Tom Smail, an Anglican clergyman and one of the founders of the Fountain Trust, in his beautiful book, *The Forgotten Father,* writes this about his own childhood and his quest for a father:

> I never knew my father. He died when I was too young to realize what I had lost but I have been discovering slowly ever since. We are all shaped by our lacks as much as by our gifts, for none of us starts complete.
>
> Tom Smail, *The Forgotten Father*

To know that you are fathered is one of the profoundest and deepest sources of confidence imaginable. It gives you a history, a place, a sense of belonging in a way that is almost inexplicable because it is so beautiful. To know that you are loved enables you to love others. It melts your heart and softens your soul. To know that you are wanted changes the way you view your place in the world. It gives you permission to be. It destroys any sense that you are simply using up air or wasting space on this planet. The impact of being fathered is depicted beautifully in Louisa May Alcott's classic novel *Little Women*:

> My child, the troubles and temptations of your life are beginning, and may be many; but you can overcome and outlive them all if you learn to feel the strength and tenderness of your Heavenly Father as you do that of your earthly one. The more you love and trust Him, the nearer you will feel to Him, and the less you will depend on human power and wisdom. His love and care never tire or change, can never be taken from you, but may become the source of lifelong peace, happiness, and strength. Believe this heartily, and go to God with all your little cares, and hopes, and sins, and sorrows, as freely and confidingly as you come to your mother.
>
> Louisa May Alcott, *Little Women*

The more you love and trust Him, the nearer you will feel to Him, and the less you will depend on human power and wisdom. This is why grasping the full significance of the first statement of the Apostles' Creed is so absolutely vital for us. When we catch it, when we realize that this conviction does not simply refer to the world and everyone around us but that it also refers to *me*, it releases us from the tyrannical grip of pointlessness and lifts us into the arms of God who loves us, nurtures us, protects us, and accepts us.

So where does this notion of a "father" come from and how do we understand it biblically?

The Old Testament – a formal and somehow "yearning" Father?

The idea of God as a father is most definitely less obvious in the Hebrew Bible and is really only used of Israel in passages such as Exodus 4:22, Deuteronomy 14:1, and Hosea 11:1–4:

> Then you shall say to Pharaoh, "Thus says the Lord: Israel is my firstborn son. I said to you, 'Let my son go that he may worship me.'"
>
> Exodus 4:22–23

> You are children of the Lord your God.
>
> Deuteronomy 14:1

> When Israel was a child, I loved him,
> and out of Egypt I called my son.
> The more I called them,
> the more they went from me;
> they kept sacrificing to the Baals,
> and offering incense to idols.
> Yet it was I who taught Ephraim to walk,
> I took them up in my arms;
> but they did not know that I healed them.
> I led them with cords of human kindness,
> with bands of love.
> I was to them like those
> who lift infants to their cheeks.
> I bent down to them and fed them.
>
> Hosea 11:1–4

God is compared to an earthly father in passages such as Psalm 103:13 and Deuteronomy 1:31 and 8:5:

> As a father has compassion for his children,
> so the Lord has compassion for those who
> fear him.
> For he knows how we were made;
> he remembers that we are dust.
>
> Psalm 103:13–14

> The Lord your God, who goes before you, is the one
> who will fight for you, just as he did for you in Egypt
> before your very eyes, and in the wilderness, where
> you saw how the Lord your God carried you, just as
> one carries a child, all the way that you travelled
> until you reached this place.
>
> Deuteronomy 1:30–31

> Know then in your heart that as a parent disciplines
> a child so the Lord your God disciplines you.
>
> Deuteronomy 8:5

The Hebrew formal term for "father" (rather like *pater* in Latin) is used on a number of occasions in the Old Testament too, sometimes in association with Israel as a nation, as in Deuteronomy 32:6, Isaiah 63:16, Jeremiah 31:9, Malachi 1:6 and 2:10, and sometimes in describing the relationship between God and the king, as in 2 Samuel 7:14, 1 Chronicles 17:13, 22:10, and 28:6, and Psalm 89:26. I have heard it argued that God is a more distant Father in the Old Testament, or that His relationship is more formal with Israel. To some extent I can understand that view, but I wonder whether it is also true to say that, despite the apparent distance and formality, God still seems to yearn for intimacy with Israel. As you read the passages that relate to His fatherly relationship with the nation, you can't help but get the impression that He is desperate for a closer relationship with them but that it is their sin and their rebellion that is creating the distance. It is not that God does not want intimacy with Israel; it is more that Israel conducts herself in such a way that she excludes herself from this intimacy. God's heart toward them is one of a loving, tender but holy Father. Their response, which is so often like ours, is that of a petulant and independent child who wants intimacy, but on their terms.

The New Testament – a new revelation of the Father's heart

There can be no doubt that the New Testament brings a completely new revelation of the depth of the father heart of God for His people. The central promise, and yearning, of God to be intimately connected to us as His people is captured in Paul's words to the Corinthians (which are based on 2 Samuel 7:14):

> And I will be your father, and you shall be my sons and daughters, says the Lord Almighty.
>
> 2 Corinthians 6:18

Paul's quotation of 2 Samuel 7:14 places the idea of God's Fatherhood firmly in the context of God's covenant relationship with David and the holiness and intimacy of the Temple. Israel longed for God to be close to them on one hand (see Isaiah 63:15, for example), but, on the other hand, as I have already said, they rejected this intimacy in favour of their own independence. Something has happened between the Old Testament and the New that now makes the longed-for intimacy of the former the promised reality and experience in the latter. That something is actually a Some*one*. It is the Lord Jesus and His ministry, message, and deliverance.

Jesus' intimacy with His Father

Jesus used an intimate and personal word for "Father" in prayer. It is the word *Abba*:

> "Abba, Father," he cried out, "everything is possible for you. Please take this cup of suffering away from me. Yet I want your will to be done, not mine."
>
> Mark 14:36 (NLT)

Perhaps one could argue that it is not particularly remarkable that Jesus would use a term of such intimacy when speaking to His Father. After all, they are clearly close. What is unfathomable, though, is that when Jesus teaches His disciples to pray He tells them that they can use the same word. It is the word *Abba*, which He uses as the opening address of what we now call the Lord's Prayer, found, among other places, in Matthew 6. Paul picks up this intimacy when he writes to the Christians in Rome and in Galatia:

> For you have not received a spirit that makes you fearful slaves. Instead, you received God's Spirit when he adopted you as his own children. Now we call him, "Abba, Father."
>
> Romans 8:15 (NLT)

> And because we are his children, God has sent the Spirit of his Son into our hearts, prompting us to call out, "Abba, Father."
>
> Galatians 4:6 (NLT)

On top of that, the word *pater*, which is seen fewer than twenty times in the Old Testament, is used more than 250 times in the New!

Father of Creation, yet Abba to those who have responded to His call in Christ

Just consider the impact of the combined messages of the New Testament about God's Fatherhood. The God who made the world, who holds all things in His power, comes to be intimately and personally connected to those who will call upon His name and trust in His grace. This concept is repeated again and again throughout the New Testament.

- It is the basis of Jesus' call to be merciful in the Sermon on the Mount and the Sermon on the Plain (see Luke 6:36; Matthew 5:45).

- It is the basis of forgiveness in Jesus' teaching just after He has cleansed the Temple in Mark's Gospel (see Mark 11:25).
- It is the very basis of prayer itself (see Matthew 6:8).
- It is the basis of trust that God will provide (see Matthew 6:32; Luke 12:30).
- It lies at the heart of how we view ourselves and other people (see Matthew 7:11; 5:44; Luke 6:36).

The teaching of Jesus to His disciples repeatedly pointed them to His Father as the source of their life, their confidence, and their hope. He came to reveal the Father to them; He did only what the Father told Him to do; He was the only way to the Father; His purpose was to accomplish His Father's will. Without the concept of God's Fatherhood at the heart of the teaching, life, and example of Jesus, God would have been as remote and difficult to access for us as He was for the Jews. Not because He does not long for intimacy, but because we would separate ourselves from Him because of our selfishness and sin, just as Israel did. A cursory glance at passages from John's Gospel and his general epistles tells us how central the purpose and the will of the Father was to the Lord Jesus (see also John 6:57; 10:30; 14:10; 10:15a; 16:15a; 1:18; 8:26–29; 12:49; 14:7, 9; and 1 John 3:1):

> The Father loves the Son and has placed all things in his hands. Whoever believes in the Son has eternal life; whoever disobeys the Son will not see life, but must endure God's wrath.
>
> John 3:35–36

Just as the living Father sent me, and I live because
of the Father, so whoever eats me will live because
of me.

John 6:57

What my Father has given me is greater than all
else, and no one can snatch it out of the Father's
hand. The Father and I are one.

John 10:29–30

Philip said to him, "Lord, show us the Father and
we will be satisfied." Jesus said to him, "Have
I been with you all this time, Philip, and you still
do not know me? Whoever has seen me has seen
the Father. How can you say, 'Show us the Father'?
Do you not believe that I am in the Father and the
Father is in me? The words that I say to you I do
not speak on my own; but the Father who dwells
in me does his works. Believe me that I am in the
Father and the Father is in me; but if you do not,
then believe me because of the works themselves."

John 14:8–12

Our relationship with God as Father flows through Jesus

Our intimacy with God the Father, however, can come
through only one source – Jesus Himself. In a number of
his epistles, Paul makes it clear that there is an indissoluble
link between our relationship with God the Father and with
the Lord Jesus Christ. Indeed, he almost always starts and

ends his letters with this basic understanding (see Romans 1:7; 1 Corinthians 1:3; 2 Corinthians 1:2; Romans 15:6; 2 Corinthians 1:3; Ephesians 1:3; Romans 15:6; 2 Corinthians 1:3). For Paul, any notion of access to God the Father is absolutely rooted in the conviction that Jesus Christ is the access point. There is no other avenue to intimacy than through the Son.

Not only that, but Paul's understanding of his own ministry is deeply linked to his notion of the Son and the Father being tied to one another, with the Son providing access to the Father. It is a fundamental part of his understanding of God and faith and how we connect to God Himself:

There is one God, the Father, from whom are all things and for whom we exist, and one Lord, Jesus Christ, through whom are all things and through whom we exist.

1 Corinthians 8:6

There is one body and one Spirit, just as you were called to the one hope of your calling, one Lord, one faith, one baptism, one God and Father of all, who is above all and through all and in all.

Ephesians 4:6

Do not get drunk with wine, for that is debauchery; but be filled with the Spirit, as you sing psalms and hymns and spiritual songs among yourselves, singing and making melody to the Lord in your hearts, giving thanks to God the Father at all times and for everything in the name of our Lord Jesus Christ.

Ephesians 5:20

There is a sense in which God is "Father of all" throughout the New Testament (see Ephesians 3:14; Hebrews 12:9; James 1:17, etc.), but there is also a sense in which God enters into a specific and adoptive relationship with those who turn to Him and submit their lives to His purposes and plans as revealed through His Son, Jesus. Many of the passages we have already explored help us to understand this, but there are two which stand out among all the words of the New Testament that help us understand the notion of God's Fatherhood more clearly than any others. They are Romans 8:14–17 and Galatians 4:1–7:

For all who are led by the Spirit of God are children of God. For you did not receive a spirit of slavery to fall back into fear, but you have received a spirit of adoption. When we cry, "Abba! Father!" it is that very Spirit bearing witness with our spirit that we are children of God, and if children, then heirs, heirs of God and joint heirs with Christ – if, in fact, we suffer with him so that we may also be glorified with him.

Romans 8:14–17

My point is this: heirs, as long as they are minors, are no better than slaves, though they are the owners of all the property; but they remain under guardians and trustees until the date set by the father. So with us; while we were minors, we were enslaved to the elemental spirits of the world. But when the fullness of time had come, God sent his Son, born of a woman, born under the law, in order to redeem those who were under the law, so that we might receive adoption as children. And because you are children, God has sent the Spirit of his Son into our hearts, crying, "Abba! Father!" So you are no longer a slave but a child, and if a child then also an heir, through God.

Galatians 4:1–17

Paul, in these two passages, paints the deep colours of what the Fatherhood of God means for those who have submitted their life to Christ. These words must have been revolutionary for Paul himself, let alone for his listeners and those who would have read his letters. He picks up the strands of Roman adoption, which cancelled all the rights of previous parents and any inheritance or bequests they might leave you and granted the full and absolute rights of inheritance, identity, and family of your new parent. He also picks up the words of intimacy and connection that flow from Jesus' use of the word *Abba*, signifying that God is intimate, present, loving, personal, and caring. Yet Paul holds on to the idea of reverence for God and respect and awe for Him with his use of the word *Abba* too. He tells the Christians in Rome and Galatia that they were *once* slaves but *now* they are *sons and daughters*. And because they are children of God their Father they are now *heirs* of all that God has given them and promises them. To seal it all, Paul reminds them that all these beautiful gifts of intimacy and grace and strength are sealed by the Holy Spirit, who lives within them, and purchased by the life and death of Christ, who rescued them.

Principles of Fatherhood

The Creed, however, does not simply say that we believe in God the Father. It says we believe in God the Father *Almighty, Creator of heaven and earth.* At the heart of Christian faith sits the conviction that God not only made us, He made the world in which we live and everything around us. We do not serve a weak and incapacitated God; we serve an *almighty* God who is able to do what He wants, when He wants, how He wants.

The concept of God the Father Almighty, the Creator of heaven and earth, implies that God has made us and the world in which we live (Genesis 1). Yet we can go further. Not only has He made us, but He has made us in His image (Genesis 1:26ff.). He upholds the Creation with *His* power yet places us as stewards within it (Genesis 2; Hebrews 1). He has made us with a purpose of love and for fellowship with Himself (John 17:23; Ephesians 3:16–17). He has not only made us, He has remade us in salvation and is remaking the planet (Romans 8; Ephesians 1). As our Father, He provides for us and sustains us (Psalm 42;

Matthew 6). As a Father He corrects us and challenges us (Hebrews 12:6; 2 Samuel 7:14). As a loving, restoring, and caring Father He will wait for us to come to Him, but when we do He will restore us to intimacy and love (Luke 15). He accepts us where we are but is committed enough to us to change us (Ephesians 1:6). In his sermon on 15 July 1883, C. H. Spurgeon, the famous British Baptist pastor, proclaimed that one of the greatest mysteries of his life was that he was "accepted of the Great Father". Surely this is also one of the greatest mysteries for us.

Unfathomable

I think if God had a mantelpiece, your picture would be on it. I think if someone asked Him to show them His family, He would pull out His wallet and show them the picture of you He carries around. I think He sends you gifts all the time to let you know He loves you. A sunrise every day, a bird's song in the evening, a breathtaking summer evening every now and then, and flowers every spring. I don't think God loves you; I *know* He does.

How could we ever hope to explain the grace and love of God to us? It is simply impossible. We don't have the words. The concept of the Creator of all things being intimately and deeply committed to you and to me is beyond our ability to comprehend, yet we can believe this unbelievable thing. And when we believe it, we are transformed. Our understanding of ourselves is changed. We no longer have anything to prove. We don't need to win people's approval. We have no test to pass to be loved by God. We do not need to change ourselves, because the work of God our Father changes us.

This is, beyond any shadow of a doubt, the greatest and most profound truth in my own life. I am accepted. I am loved. I am cherished. That changes everything. There will be many reading these words who do not sense that acceptance. You wonder whether God could love you. Whether the idea of His being a father could possibly apply to you. Well, it does. He will not force Himself upon us. He will not manipulate and control us, but He will wait for us and when we turn to Him He will run to us and restore us.

God loves us enough to change us too. There is a dangerous and grace-weakening idea that God doesn't want to change you. You can stay as you are and do as you please. That is neither biblical nor liberating. God loves us enough to change us. To clean us, to restore us. I love this little story from American pastor and author Max Lucado:

> When my daughter was a toddler, I used to take her to a park not far from our apartment. One day as she was playing in a sandbox, an ice-cream salesman approached us. I purchased her a treat, and when I turned to give it to her, I saw her mouth was full of sand. Where I had intended to put a delicacy, she had put dirt.

Did I love her with dirt in her mouth? Absolutely. Was she any less of my daughter with dirt in her mouth? Of course not. Was I going to allow her to keep the dirt in her mouth? No way. I loved her right where she was, but I refused to leave her there. I carried her over to the water fountain and washed out her mouth. Why? Because I love her.

God does the same for us. He holds us over the fountain. "Spit out the dirt, honey," our Father urges. "I've got something better for you." And so he cleanses us of filth: immorality, dishonesty, prejudice, bitterness, greed. We don't enjoy the cleansing; sometimes we even opt for the dirt over the ice cream. "I can eat dirt if I want to!" we pout and proclaim. Which is true – we can. But if we do, the loss is ours. God has a better offer.

Max Lucado, *Just Like Jesus*

Does God love us where we are? Of course He does! Does He father us there? Of course He does! Will He leave us there? Absolutely not. We can have confidence that He will wash out our mouths. We weren't made to wallow in the dirt; we were made for holiness. We weren't made for death; we were made for life. We weren't made to manage; we were made to radiate His glory – and if we give Him the raw materials of our lives, we can have confidence that He will change our lives and use us for His purposes.

One last thought. The nineteenth-century politician and diplomat Charles Francis Adams kept a diary. One day he entered:

Went fishing with my son today – a day wasted.

His son, Brook, also kept a diary, which is still in existence. On that same day, Brook Adams made this entry:

Went fishing with my father – the most wonderful day of my life!

The father thought he was wasting his time while fishing with his son, but his son saw it as an investment of time. The only way to tell the difference between wasting and investing is to know one's ultimate purpose in life and to judge accordingly.

Isn't it ironic that many of us who are fathers make the same mistake? Let's not do it any more. But isn't it even more ironic that we have a Father who would love to "go fishing" with us and we are often the ones who say to God, "What a waste of time!"

God the Father Almighty, Creator of heaven and earth...

Do I believe this for the world?

Do I believe it for myself?

God made me? *Really?* God doesn't make mistakes. He makes all things beautiful. That means I'm not a mistake. That means I'm beautiful. You will never have any idea how liberating those words are to me as I write them on the page.

I am not a mistake. Neither are you. You're loved. You're wanted. You're cherished.

Blows your mind, doesn't it?

Unbelievable...

Chapter Six

Unbeatable:
I believe in Jesus Christ, His only Son, our Lord...

I believe in Jesus Christ, his only Son, our Lord.
He was conceived by the power of the Holy Spirit
and born of the Virgin Mary.
He suffered under Pontius Pilate,
was crucified, died, and was buried.
He descended to the dead.
On the third day he rose again.
He ascended into heaven,
and is seated at the right hand of the Father.
He will come again to judge the living and the dead.

She will bear a son, and you are to name him Jesus, for he
will save his people from their sins.

Matthew explaining who Jesus was and how His birth came about
Matthew 1:21

...Christ Jesus... though he was in the form of God, did not
regard equality with God as something to be exploited,
but emptied himself, taking the form of a slave, being born
in human likeness. And being found in human form, he
humbled himself and became obedient to the point of death
– even death on a cross. Therefore God also highly exalted

him and gave him the name that is above every name,
so that at the name of Jesus every knee should bend, in
heaven and on earth and under the earth, and every tongue
should confess that Jesus Christ is Lord, to the glory of
God the Father.

Paul to the Christians in Philippi
Philippians 2:5–11

Christianity doesn't work without Jesus.

I know it might sound like a very obvious thing to say, but it is nevertheless true.

It's a bit like trying to have life without breath, or a heartbeat without a heart. All Christians would, I think, acknowledge that Christ is the centre of gravity of their faith. Just as the earth revolves around the sun, so Christians should orientate their lives around Jesus.

Simple, right?

Maybe not quite as simple as that.

The issue for us Christians is not whether or not we believe in Jesus. I would take that as a given. The issue really is who is the Jesus that we believe in? You would be surprised how many different versions of Jesus there are out there.

I recently had a conversation with a devout follower of Jesus who was absolutely convinced that the Jesus she followed was a wealthy man who never faced financial struggle. Why? Because the wise men at His birth gave Him gold, and He and His family had invested it. I asked her what she thought of the idea that Jesus Himself had said

113

that He didn't even have anywhere to live, and she said that wasn't relevant. The truth was that she had been taught in her Church that no Christian should ever be poor, sick or struggling, and therefore she had been introduced to a Jesus who fitted the required description.

Or what about another friend of mine? He told me that Jesus never challenged anyone to change their life. He accepted them and affirmed them right where they were and there was never any expectation of change. Really, I asked? Is that really what Jesus was like? Didn't He challenge the rich young ruler to sell all he owned? Didn't He ask His disciples to take up a cross and follow Him? Didn't He challenge the woman at the well about her sexual behaviour? What about the religious leaders or the moneychangers? When He met the apostle Paul, didn't He challenge him? I was reading too much into the text, he said. I suggested he might not be reading the text enough.

Another friend told me she believed that Jesus was only interested in "saving souls". He wasn't interested in feeding the poor, clothing the naked, or caring for the sick. Yet He made sure His disciples had meals. He asked them to feed the people who were listening to Him, and when they couldn't do it, He did. He told His disciples that they *had* to care for the prisoner and clothe the naked and give those who had nowhere to stay a roof over their heads. He spent nearly all of His time with the poor and the forgotten and the outcasts. That might be true, she said, but He only did that so that they would be converted. His was only a spiritual mission, she argued. I don't think that's right.

The great theologian Karl Barth once said that we were guilty of making God in our own image. He had a point. We craft and fashion Jesus according to what we would like Him to be, instead of what He really was. We turn Him into either a bigger version or a nicer version of ourselves. That's always a mistake. If we are not careful, we end up with a Jesus who agrees with everything we stand for. I guess Martin Luther was right. Sin really is the heart curved in upon itself, and we are all guilty of making Jesus "fit into" our lives, our cultures, and our preferences.

Here's the problem. Jesus will never "fit into" our lives. Like it or not, we have a flesh-and-blood Jesus that we have to deal with. God didn't come to us in a series of concepts, ideas, and words. He came as a man. He lived on this planet. He breathed our air. He faced our challenges. We can't create a magical Jesus out of thin air to suit our needs and to pander to our desires. He doesn't ask us if He can fit into our plans. He shows us what God is like, reveals God's purposes and plans for the world, instigates God's Kingdom, and then asks us whether we want to follow Him or not.

He'll go out of His way to meet us, to engage with us, and to talk with us, but He won't change His overall purpose and plan for anyone. He knows what He is doing and invites us to join Him and allows us the freedom of saying no. The task is clear, the offer is made, and the work has started. He wants us to travel with Him, to follow Him, to be part of His band of world-changers, but He isn't going to soften the task, weaken the commitment, or change the great plan of God for you or for me.

It is this flesh-and-blood Jesus, this actual Saviour, that we must grapple with. God confronts us in the physical ministry and message of Jesus. In the earthy and uncomfortable reality of a carpenter from Nazareth. Christian faith just doesn't make sense without the real and physical and actual Jesus of the New Testament. In his book *The Furious Longing of God,* author Brennan Manning wrote:

> The gospel is absurd and the life of Jesus is meaningless unless we believe that He lived, died, and rose again with but one purpose in mind: to make brand-new creation. Not to make people with better morals but to create a community of prophets and professional lovers, men and women who would surrender to the mystery of the fire of the Spirit that burns within, who would live in ever greater fidelity to the omnipresent Word of God, who would enter into the center of it all, the very heart and mystery of Christ, into the center of the flame that consumes, purifies, and sets everything aglow with peace, joy, boldness, and extravagant, furious love. This, my friend, is what it really means to be a Christian.
>
> Brennan Manning, *The Furious Longing of God*

If we are not free to make Jesus look as we want Him to look and say what we want Him to say, how do we handle the Jesus we encounter in the New Testament? Eduard Schweizer, in his 1987 book *Jesus Christ: The Man from Nazareth and the Exalted Lord,* asks penetrating questions:

Who is this man whose authority commands illness and obsession? Who is this man who claims that following him is the one decisive act in view of the coming kingdom, more important than caring for one's family and providing food for them? Who is this man who acts as if he were the almighty God himself, who alone has the authority to forgive sins? Who is this man who thinks that God's kingdom has been actualized in his words and deeds? Who is this man who sees in himself the manifestation of God's kingdom? Who is this man who thinks that failing to respond to him is worse than any other sin? Who is this man who puts himself on a plane equal to or even superior to the God of the Bible?...

Who is this man? Obviously, a harmless Jesus, a mere prophet or teacher or moral example, will not suffice. Either he was a case of religious mania, living in illusions and dreams of being the incarnation of God's sovereignty on earth, or he was exactly this. However, if he <u>was</u> exactly this, we must also say that he <u>is</u> exactly this. Is he?...

A belief in Jesus that does not include the whole of his preaching and his work – that is, a belief that would not be "stamped" by the life and death of Jesus of Nazareth – would not be real faith.

Eduard Schweizer, *Jesus Christ: The Man from Nazareth and the Exalted Lord*

It strikes me that if we are to have confidence in Jesus today, we must, to the best of our ability, return to the Jesus we discover in the Gospels and in the pages of the New Testament. Any attempts to change Him to make Him "fit into" our culture will actually fundamentally weaken our confidence in Him. I am not talking about a return to the "cut-and-paste" approach to the New Testament that was employed by the early Christian called Marcion, nor am I suggesting a rush to nineteenth-century German liberal theology that takes all the miraculous incidents in Jesus' life out of the story. Such enterprises not only rip up the accounts of Jesus, they also rip up any trust we might have in the authentic and authenticated stories and words of the Bible. I am not even talking about the modern "Red-Letter" movements, which try to focus on what Jesus said only (and can sound just like Marcion but with modern accents).

No, I am talking about returning to the *actual* Jesus we encounter in the New Testament and letting Him speak for Himself. Letting His miracles stand as miracles. Letting His parables stand as parables. Letting His life stand as His life. I am talking about understanding the context and the culture of Jesus' words and life and ministry as much as possible, but allowing Him to be Himself. As we discover the Jesus we encounter in the New Testament, I think our response might be the same as that of those who listened to Him during His earthly ministry:

Now when Jesus had finished saying these things, the crowds were astounded at his teaching, for he taught them as one having authority, and not as their scribes.

Matthew 7:28–29

Jesus in the Apostles' Creed and the implications for today

And so we come to the words of the Apostles' Creed about Jesus:

I believe in Jesus Christ, his only Son, our Lord.
He was conceived by the power of the Holy Spirit
and born of the Virgin Mary.
He suffered under Pontius Pilate,
was crucified, died, and was buried.
He descended to the dead.
On the third day he rose again.
He ascended into heaven,
and is seated at the right hand of the Father.
He will come again to judge the living and the
dead.

These words were part of a long and protracted discussion about who Jesus actually was, and the context of their formation has a great deal to say to us today. The first few hundred years of the Church's life saw a series of heated debates about who Jesus really was. The pendulum swung from one extreme to the other. Was He really human or did He just appear to be human, as Docetism believed? Was He really God, equal with the Father, or was He less than the Father in some way, subordinate to Him, as Arianism believed? Are the Father, the Son, and the Holy Spirit all one God who just appears differently at different points in time and history, as Sabellianism believed, or do the Father, the Son, and the Holy Spirit all exist as one God in three different expressions, but all equal in power and substance and all eternally present together in the Trinity?

You may think that such questions are irrelevant to the matter of our confidence in our faith, but this is not so. The Apostles' Creed was formulated *at least in part* to address the core question of what God is actually like, and the section we are exploring now was addressing a vital part of that – was Jesus God or was He human? Or was He both? The answer to this question changed everything for the Christians in the third century. The Church was seeking to understand the life and ministry of Jesus because they wanted to be faithful to Him. Had Jesus Christ truly understood Himself to be God? Did the Second Person of the Trinity genuinely take up flesh and live among people or not? If He did not, then the life of Jesus was a mirage, a picture or a metaphor that helped us understand God but did not actually involve God coming to earth in human form. On the other hand, if God did come to live among us, then in what way was He still God? What did He give up, if anything, of His nature?

These questions were deeply important then and they are still deeply important now. At their heart are the issues of whether God truly understands us. Has He really sent His Son to rescue us? Can we relate to Jesus? Can we trust Him? Is He just "a" way or is He "the" way? These deep and powerful formative discussions may have taken place in Nicea and Constantinople and Alexandria and Jerusalem in the early years of the Church's life, but they are still taking place today – in Mecca and Jerusalem. They are discussion points in Brixton and Harlem. They form conversations in Rome. Is Jesus the Son of God or is He not? Is He human or not? Is He divine or not? Can we have confidence in the Jesus we encounter in the Bible?

Can we change Him to fit the culture or does He stand and ask the culture to change?

The power of the Apostles' Creed about Jesus

Read the confession from the Creed about Jesus again – slowly.

> I believe in Jesus Christ, his only Son, our Lord.
> He was conceived by the power of the Holy Spirit
> and born of the Virgin Mary.
> He suffered under Pontius Pilate,
> was crucified, died, and was buried.
> He descended to the dead.
> On the third day he rose again.
> He ascended into heaven,
> and is seated at the right hand of the Father.
> He will come again to judge the living and the
>   dead.

These words articulate the historic, orthodox, and accepted teaching of the Church through the ages on the person, ministry, and purpose of Jesus Christ. They are staggering. If I were to write about each line of the Apostles' Creed, it would take ten books of this size to work my way through it, and maybe that would not be a bad thing. Every single phrase of this statement packs a theological punch that made it clear to those who were trying to argue otherwise that Jesus Christ was a powerful and clear articulation of God Himself.

Jesus is the Messiah – our Lord and our Deliverer sent from God

- *Jesus is the Christ* – the Messiah, the long-awaited Deliverer. He is rooted in the story of the Old Testament and springs from the Jewish story.
- He is the *only Son* of God – this phrase would go on to require greater clarification, which would be given in the Declaration of Chalcedon. Jesus is the unique revelation of God to us. He is the Son. Chalcedon and Nicea describe Him as "God of God, very God of very God". He is not simply "like God"; He is God. He is not just "a version"; he is God.
- He is *our Lord* – Jesus demands allegiance, obedience, and faithfulness from all who would claim to be His followers.

Jesus carries both divinity and humanity

- *He was conceived by the power of the Holy Spirit.* The story is true. His paternity did not come through a man, but through God Himself.
- *Born of the Virgin Mary* – just as was prophesied in the book of Isaiah, Jesus' mother was a virgin when He was born. This leads to the inevitable conclusion that He was both divine and human.

Jesus' death was physical and actual

- *He suffered under Pontius Pilate.* This was not a "conceptual" or a "metaphorical" death. It was actual, located in time and history. He came to a specific time, place, and context.
- *Was crucified, died, and was buried.* Jesus endured complete and full humiliation, human suffering, and death. His death led to His body being taken down from the tree and He was placed as a lifeless corpse in a tomb.

While dead, Jesus fulfilled a ministry of deliverance

- *He descended to the dead.* This emphasizes that Jesus did not simply "rest" in the tomb. With His body dead and in the tomb, Jesus entered the land of the dead and broke its chains.

Jesus did not stay dead, but instead defeated death

- *On the third day, he rose from the dead.* Jesus Christ is not the only person to have come back from the dead, but He is the only person to have come back from the dead and into a new and glorified body, which He still inhabits and will never leave. That is why the New Testament describes Him as the "first born from among the dead" or the "last Adam". His resurrection was full and complete. It was not a mirage, it was not a trick, and it was not a metaphor.

Jesus now continues to fulfil His ministry of intercession

- *He ascended into heaven and is seated at the right hand of the Father.* Jesus may not be visible now, but He is certainly alive and active in heaven. This tells us that heaven is not just a concept or an altered dimension; it is a reality that we cannot see, but it is nevertheless as real as our world is. Jesus is there now and is carrying out a kingly and priestly ministry of intercession.

Jesus will come again as Judge

- *He will come again to judge the living and the dead.* The ministry of Jesus is not over. He will return, and when He does He will come as a judge before whom all the people who have ever lived will stand.

These historic and confessed truths sit at the heart of orthodox Christianity not simply because we learn them from the Apostles' Creed, however. Rather, they are articulated in the Creed because Christians believed these things to be true. They were the truths evidenced in the Gospels, and collected in the epistles. Remember that the Apostles' Creed was formulated on the basis of the old Roman Creed. The former emerged around AD 390, but the latter was in circulation in some form from the end of the first century. By the time the Creed we are familiar with had emerged, it was being used to teach baptismal candidates what lies at the heart of the Church's teaching about Christ. The developing canon of Scripture supported these truths.

Of course there are massive things that the Creed does not include. No mention of the Jews? No mention of the life of Jesus? No mention of the Kingdom of God? I would argue that these matters are addressed by implication in these statements, but that is for another book. I asked a question at the beginning of this chapter about what kind of Jesus we believed in. The Creed gives us the Jesus we believe in. It shows us the Jesus that the Church tries to serve. He is there in the words.

The Jesus of the Church is the one who is the only Son of God, the Messiah and Deliverer who came to earth conceived by the power of the Holy Spirit and embedded in the womb of a virgin. He is human and divine simultaneously and He actually lived and walked and suffered and died among us at a specific time and in a specific place. His body was taken from a cross and placed in a tomb because He was dead, but He broke the chains of death, and three days after dying He rose again and then ascended to His Father in heaven. He is there now and will one day return, and every person who has ever lived will stand before Him and He will be their judge.

This is the heart of the historic Christian faith about Jesus. We cannot and should not change it. This is the Jesus we believe in. This is the Jesus who redeems us. This is the Saviour that we need, even if He is not always the Saviour that we want. This is the benchmark against which we measure the words of theologians, pastors, Christians, scholars, authors, and writers. It is this Jesus who is the Saviour of the Church. This Jesus and no other. This is the tangible Jesus.

We have no need to guess what Jesus was like; we have a plethora of eyewitness accounts and stories and deep reflections on Him from those who walked with Him, as well as further writings by those who became His followers within a short time after His ascension. We also have an assurance that Jesus *faithfully* reflects the personality and character of God to us. If we want to know what God is like, we can see Him very clearly in the life and ministry of the Second Person of the Trinity.

Eyewitness accounts and the biblical narrative

The New Testament is an accurate and reliable account of the life and ministry of Jesus of Nazareth. Despite the fact that there is an increased tendency to try to dismiss elements of the story of Jesus' life and impact on many parts of the Church's life today, we are told in the Bible itself that the stories it recounts are reliable and trustworthy (in addition, see Acts 11:4; 2 Timothy 4:5, 17 and Mark 1:1):

> Since many have undertaken to set down an orderly account of the events that have been fulfilled among us, just as they were handed on to us by those who from the beginning were eyewitnesses and servants of the word, I too decided, after investigating everything carefully from the very first, to write an orderly account for you, most excellent Theophilus, so that you may know the truth concerning the things about which you have been instructed.
>
> Luke 1:1-4

> In the first book, Theophilus, I wrote about all that Jesus did and taught from the beginning until the day when he was taken up to heaven, after giving instructions through the Holy Spirit to the apostles whom he had chosen. After his suffering he presented himself alive to them by many convincing proofs, appearing to them over the course of forty days and speaking about the kingdom of God...
>
> Acts 1:1-3

> You also are to testify because you have been with me from the beginning.
>
> John 15:27

Now Jesus did many other signs in the presence of his disciples, which are not written in this book. But these are written so that you may come to believe that Jesus is the Messiah, the Son of God, and that through believing you may have life in his name.

John 20:30–31

This is the disciple who is testifying to these things and has written them, and we know that his testimony is true. But there are also many other things that Jesus did; if every one of them were written down, I suppose that the world itself could not contain the books that would be written.

John 21:24

...we cannot keep from speaking about what we have seen and heard...

Acts 4:20

For we did not follow cleverly devised myths when we made known to you the power and coming of our Lord Jesus Christ, but we had been eyewitnesses of his majesty.

2 Peter 1:16

John to the seven churches that are in Asia: Grace to you and peace from him who is and who was and who is to come, and from the seven spirits who are before his throne, and from Jesus Christ, the

faithful witness, the firstborn of the dead, and the
ruler of the kings of the earth.

Revelation 1:4-5

There is also a sense in the Bible of the whole story being
affirmed and an invitation to the reader or listener to engage
with the Bible with an assurance that it is God's word to His
people and that it is given to strengthen us and to build our
faith (see also Romans 15:4 and 2 Peter 1:20–21):

All scripture is inspired by God and is useful for
teaching, for reproof, for correction and for training
in righteousness, so that everyone who belongs to
God may be proficient, equipped for every good work.

2 Timothy 3:16-17

You cannot help but get the feeling that the writers of the
various elements of the Bible knew that they were involved
in something that was much bigger and more important
than themselves. They were part of a culture that took
accurate records and the passing on of information
extremely seriously and they went out of their way to
ensure that what they said was an accurate reflection of
what they had been told. The writers of Scripture set out to
be faithful in their own recording of God's word to them,
and this increases our own ability to trust that the content
of the Bible is reliable.

129

God in flesh and blood – beyond an idea

The powerful story of the Gospels tells us of the actual Jesus who lived and breathed and walked in first-century Israel. He is not a concept or an idea, but a Person. We must not underestimate the significance of the incarnation. The Second Person of the Trinity came into an *actual* context. He had to learn to walk and sit at the table. He was taught a trade by Joseph, His earthly father. When His public ministry began, people were astonished by Him and taken aback by His words, precisely because many of them still thought of Him as "the carpenter's son":

> Coming to his home town, he began teaching the people in their synagogue, and they were amazed. "Where did this man get this wisdom and these miraculous powers?" they asked. "Isn't this the carpenter's son? Isn't his mother's name Mary, and aren't his brothers James, Joseph, Simon and Judas? Aren't all his sisters with us? Where then did this man get all these things?"
>
> Matthew 13:54–56 (NIV)

At the heart of Christianity we see not just an idea of God, but a Person who shows us what God is like – the Lord Jesus. His interactions with people, His struggles with temptation, His engagement with religious authorities, His practice of prayer, His example – these are all real and tangible. He is the only figure in any religion to claim not simply to point to a way of life, but to *be* that way. His words about Himself,

130

evidenced in His character, His behaviour, and His ministry, are astounding.

The concrete challenge of Jesus' life and example confronts us and inspires us on a daily basis. This is wonderfully illustrated in Charles M. Sheldon's novel *In His Steps*, in which the famous *What Would Jesus Do?* phrase originates. The story recounts the impact of the simple decision to follow Jesus and the challenges this choice presents. A revolution is sparked in the First Church of Raymond when the Revd Henry Maxwell is confronted by a young man who has hit hard times. Here's how Sheldon describes this fictional Church on the Sunday when everything began to change:

> The First Church of Raymond believed in having the best music that money could buy, and its quarter choir this morning was a source of great pleasure to the congregation. The anthem was inspiring. All the music was in keeping with the subject of the sermon...
>
> Charles Sheldon, *In His Steps*

As the service continues, everything is very nice and respectable until the young man, who had been to visit Revd Maxwell just a few days before, walks to the front of the Church at the end of the sermon. The visitor to the Church has lost his wife and is struggling to try to get his little daughter back. The book is set at the time of the Great Depression, when the suffering he is enduring was widespread across American society. Referring to the message that Revd Maxwell had just preached, the desperate young father speaks to the entire congregation, saying:

"... I was wondering as I sat there under the gallery, if what you call following Jesus is the same thing as what He taught. What did He mean when He said: 'Follow me!'? The minister said," here the man turned about and looked up at the pulpit: "that it is necessary for the disciple of Jesus to follow His steps, and he said the steps are obedience, faith, love and imitation. But I did not hear him tell you just what he meant that to mean, especially the last step. What do you Christians mean by following the steps of Jesus?... What do you mean when you sing, 'I'll go with Him, with Him all the way?' Do you mean that you are suffering and denying yourselves and trying to save lost, suffering humanity just as I understand Jesus did? What do you mean by it? I see the ragged edge of things a good deal. I understand there are more than five hundred men in this city in my case. Most of them have families. My wife died four months ago. I'm glad she is out of trouble. My little girl is staying with a printer's family until I find a job. Somehow I get puzzled when I see so many Christians living in luxury and singing, 'Jesus, I my cross have taken, all to leave and follow Thee', and remember how my wife died in New York City, gasping for air and asking God to take the little girl too. Of course I don't expect you people can prevent every one from dying of starvation, lack of proper nourishment and tenement air, but what does following Jesus mean? I understand that Christian people own a good many tenements. A member of a church was the owner of the one where my wife died, and I have wondered if following Jesus all the way was true in his case... It seems to me there's an awful lot of trouble in the world that somehow wouldn't exist at all if all the people who sing such songs went and lived them out. I suppose I don't understand. But what would Jesus do? Is that what you mean by following His steps? It seems to me sometimes as if the people in the big churches had good clothes and nice houses to live in, and money to spend for luxuries, and could go away on summer vacations and all that, while the people outside the churches, thousands of them, I mean, die in tenements, and walk the streets for jobs, and never have a piano or a picture in the house, and grow up in misery and drunkenness and sin."

Charles Sheldon, *In His Steps*

The reality is that such a question does not need to be answered with theories or ideas or hypotheses. Jesus shows us what to do because He tangibly and evidently lived, walked, died, and rose again. Perhaps the question should be "What *did* Jesus do?" rather than "What would Jesus do?".

It is easy for us to turn our spirituality into a set of "what ifs" and "maybes" and "perhaps I coulds", but the clear, evident, and uncomfortable reality for us is that the incarnation does not give us such an option. If following Jesus does not look like the tangible Jesus, then how on earth can we claim to be following Him at all?

Three people who were convinced by the story of Scripture

There have been many people who have sought to prove that the story of Jesus as recorded in the Bible is inaccurate. Three such people were Frank Morison, Lee Strobel, and Josh McDowell. They each tell their own story.

Frank Morison was a lawyer who wrote the book *Who Moved the Stone?* and first published it in 1930. He was convinced that the story of the resurrection wasn't true, but, as he studied it, he realized that he was wrong. The book tells the story of how the facts of Jesus' death and resurrection changed his mind. In his explanation for the book he writes:

> I need not stay to describe here how, fully ten years later, the opportunity came to study the life of Christ as I had long wanted to study it, investigate the origins of its literature, to sift some of the evidence at first hand, and to form my own judgment on the problem which it presents. I will only say that it effected a revolution in my thought. Things emerged from that old-world story which

previously I should have thought impossible. Slowly, but very definitely, the conviction grew that the drama of those unforgettable weeks of human history was stranger and deeper than it seemed. It was the strangeness of many notable things in the story which first arrested and held my interest. It was only later that the irresistible logic of their meaning came into view.

Frank Morison, *Who Moved the Stone?*

Josh McDowell wrote *Evidence that Demands a Verdict* in 1972. He has written a number of additions to the book since then. He, similarly, set out to disprove the story of Christ's life, death, and resurrection. He wrote:

Is the Bible historically reliable? Is there credible evidence of Christ's claim to be God? Will Christianity stand up before 21ˢᵗ Century critics? Yes.

Josh McDowell, *Evidence that Demands a Verdict*

Lee Strobel wrote *The Case for Christ* in 1998. As a journalist, he had set out to disprove the story of Jesus' life, death, and resurrection but was confronted with the reality of Christ's life, death and resurrection. In a later book, entitled *The Case for Faith*, he wrote this:

To be honest, I didn't want to believe that Christianity could radically transform someone's character and values. It was much easier to raise doubts and manufacture outrageous objections than to consider the possibility that God actually could trigger a revolutionary turn-around in such a depraved and degenerate life.

Lee Strobel, *The Case for Faith*

Each of these men changed their minds about Jesus after they had read the Bible. They came to the Bible to prove Jesus' claims were false, but they left convinced that they were true. It is only the Jesus whom we encounter in Scripture that provides such confidence for us as we seek to live out our faith in the twenty-first century.

His faithfulness to the actual character and heart of God

The second aspect of the "tangible" nature of the Lord Jesus is that He accurately reflects what God is like to us.

The incarnation is not a last-ditch attempt to show us God; it is a full revelation of what God is *actually* like. In it, we clearly see hitherto hidden or only partially revealed aspects of God's character and heart.

This is surely one of the most powerful and challenging aspects of the ministry and purpose of God's Son for us. He comes to us, while we are still fallen and lost (Romans 5). He shows us what God is like (Colossians 1). He reveals God's heart to us (John 17:25–26). He mixes and mingles with people whom Israel has shunned and ostracized up to this point (Luke 15). He tells His disciples that, when they have seen Him, they have seen the Father (John 14). He speaks of God in intimate and personal ways that would have shocked and angered the Pharisees and the scribes (Matthew 6). He forgives sins (Luke 5). He accepts worship (Matthew 14:33; John 9:38). He claims ultimate authority (Matthew 28:16–20). He speaks of God in ways that Israel has never heard before (see the "I am" sayings of John's Gospel in 6:35; 8:12; 10:9, 11; 11:25; 14:6; 15:1).

There is perhaps no clearer articulation of this sense of Jesus *authentically* and *comprehensively* representing God to us than in the words Paul uses to the believers in Colossae. In his short letter to this fledgling Church, Paul emphasizes again and again that, in Christ, they see what God is really like (see also Colossians 1:27; 2:2–5, 6–15; 3:1–4):

He is the image of the invisible God, the firstborn of all creation; for in him all things in heaven and on earth were created, things visible and invisible, whether thrones or dominions or rulers or powers – all things have been created through him and for him. He himself is before all things and in him all things hold together. He is the head of the body, the church; he is the beginning, the firstborn from the dead, so that he might come to have first place in everything. For in him all the fullness of God was pleased to dwell, and through him God was pleased to reconcile to himself all things, whether on earth or in heaven, by making peace through the blood of his cross.

Colossians 1:15–20

Let Jesus be who He claimed to be

So, as we look at Christ, we see what God is really like. We must be careful, however, to let Him speak for Himself, rather than put words into His mouth. Jesus asked His own disciples who the people around them thought that He was, and then He asked them directly as His followers who *they* thought He was (Matthew 16). Some thought He was a prophet, some thought He was Elijah brought back to life, others thought He was a mysterious figure. Peter answered Jesus' question directly:

> You are the Messiah, the Son of the living God.
>
> Matthew 16:16

Despite protestations to the contrary, Jesus' claims for Himself were profound and challenging, not just for His own day but also for ours. There are implicit claims in His public life and ministry that He is divine:

- He claims to be the Messiah, or the Deliverer of Israel (John 4; 10:22–42).
- He describes Himself as the Son of God (John 10:36).
- He equates Himself to God when the devil tempts Him (Matthew 4:7; Luke 4:12).
- He asserts that He has greater authority than Moses and attributes the voice and authority of God to His own words (Matthew 5:21–22, 27–28, 31–32, 33–34, 38–39, 43–44).
- He equates His "lordship" with God's (Matthew 7:21–22; Luke 6:46).

- He forgives sin – only God can do that (Matthew 9:2; Mark 2:5; Luke 5:20; 7:48).

- He describes Himself as Lord of the Sabbath (Matthew 12:8; Mark 2:28; Luke 6:5) and therefore Lord of the "Law".

- He promises that where two or three gather in His name He will be there – a claim to omnipresence; He also promises never to leave His disciples (Matthew 18:20; 28:16–20).

- He refers to Himself as "the Lord" (Matthew 21:3; Luke 19:31–34).

- He acknowledges that He is "the Son of God" (Luke 22:70).

- He uses the intimate word *Abba* for His Father (Mark 14:36).

- Luke reports Jesus instructing a man to tell of all that God had done for him (Luke 8:39).

- Jesus describes Himself as God when the one leper returns to thank Him for healing him (Luke 17:18).

- Jesus clearly identifies Himself with the Messiah on His entry into Jerusalem (Luke 19:38, 40).

- Jesus clearly equates Himself with God to the extent that the Jews are outraged (John 5, NB v. 18).

You cannot read the New Testament in any depth without realizing that Jesus makes the boldest and most audacious claim imaginable to the audience around Him. He is no less than God who has come to them, to reach out the hand of hope and friendship. He is the King who has come to establish His Kingdom. He is the Messiah who has come to deliver His people. He is the Son of God, the Son of Man. He is the One who brings life, hope, and deliverance with Him. He is to be worshipped, adored, and followed. Yet He comes as a carpenter, with no great possessions.

Personal encounter and His power at work in our lives today

People continue to be changed by the power of Jesus. His life and ministry continue to have an impact on millions and millions of people across the world who follow Him. There is something quite remarkable about the power of God working through the life and example of Jesus to change lives.

The Bible itself is full of stories of lives transformed by an encounter with Jesus. From those He called to follow Him (for example Matthew 4:18–21) to those He healed and delivered (for example Matthew 8), every page of the Gospels overflows with the life-changing power of Jesus tangibly evidenced in people's lives.

In his book *Encounters with Jesus*, Tim Keller speaks of the power of Jesus' encounters with people and the way it has affected Keller's own life and ministry:

> I still accept the authority of all of the Bible, and love learning and teaching from all of it. But I first felt the personal weight of the Bible's spiritual authority in the Gospels, particularly in those conversations Jesus had with individuals... I suppose you could

say that many of my own formative encounters with Jesus came from studying his encounters with individuals in the Gospels.

Tim Keller, *Encounters with Jesus*

The Church that I lead is full of people who have been changed by the power and the grace of God as seen and encountered through Jesus. Any local Church has people whose whole destiny and understanding have been transformed by an encounter with Jesus.

Jesus Christ is still tangibly and powerfully transforming lives today. He has changed my life. He may well have changed yours. He is still present in the world through His people, and He now calls us to be His hands and feet in our workplaces, our homes, our schools, our universities, and our communities. His tangible power is at work across generations, cultures, and societies.

Bilquis Sheikh recounts the story of her conversion from Islam to Christianity in her book, *I Dared to Call Him Father*. She speaks of the power of encountering Jesus and the truth of who He is. As she read the Christian Scriptures, she recalls,

Something happened to me as I went through the book; instead of reading the Bible, I found myself living it.

Bilquis Sheikh, *I Dared to Call Him Father*

Catherine Campbell comes from Northern Ireland. She and her husband, Philip, had three children – Cheryl, Paul, and

Joy. Both Cheryl and Joy were born with multiple disabilities, and both died. Catherine tells her story in her book *Under the Rainbow,* and I have rarely read such a moving account of faith in the face of loss. It was Catherine's faith in Jesus that carried her through:

> For a period of almost twenty years, God had allowed me to care for our two beautiful, brave daughters. I have never stopped being their mother; it is just that now we cannot be together for a while. They, however, continue to bless my life every day that I live. I would be lying if I said that I wouldn't have changed a thing, for what mother would deliberately choose suffering for her children? What I wouldn't change, however, is the perspective that having Cheryl and Joy has added to my thinking. I can now value people for who they are, and not merely for what they can do. And I am utterly convinced that life here pales into insignificance in comparison with what lies ahead for those who love Christ. Neither would I have wanted to miss all that I have learned about God, and from God. It has been both priceless and precious.
>
> Catherine Campbell, *Under the Rainbow*

Sheridan Voysey is an Australian writer and broadcaster who lives in the UK. He and his wife, Merryn, are unable to have children. He writes hauntingly and beautifully of their journey in his book *Resurrection Year,* and of how faith in Jesus has held them and strengthened them for the years ahead:

> After forty years in the wilderness, the Jews entered the Promised Land.
> After forty days in the wilderness, Jesus launched his world-changing mission and this gives me hope as I look out over Abingdon Road.
> After the wilderness comes a new beginning...
>
> Sheridan Voysey, *Resurrection Year*

Barnabas Mam has been the regional director in Asia for Ambassadors for Christ International since 2007. He is a Cambodian and joined the Communist party as a teenager. He was converted to Christ while spying on a Christian evangelistic meeting in the early 1970s. He was later arrested and sent to the Killing Fields, where he spent four years in captivity. After his release, Barnabas was forced to flee the country and he spent another eight years in a refugee camp in Thailand. After returning home, Barnabas helped rebuild the Church in Cambodia and he has been involved in planting over 400 Churches since. In his book, *Church Behind the Wire*, he writes this of a conversation he had with his father, who was a Buddhist, about Barnabas's own new-found faith in Christ:

> Dad, just like I've said before, Jesus is in my heart. I can worship Him anywhere. If everything is taken away, I will worship Him on the back of a water

buffalo. I will worship Him in the branches of a tree. I will worship Him while rowing a boat. He is everywhere.

Barnabas Mam, *Church Behind the Wire*

Unbreakable

We do not need to look very far to see tangible evidence of Jesus. Perhaps we need only look at what we have become or at the person sitting next to us in Church. We can have enormous confidence in the grace and power of God at work through His Son, Jesus, because the Jesus we meet in the Bible is the Jesus who is changing the world today.

His birth, His life, His death, His resurrection, His ascension, His promised return. They all give us deep confidence. Yet, somehow, it is His resurrection that makes the rest of it make sense, don't you think? If Jesus had done all the glorious things He did but then had *stayed dead*, the rest of the story would have fallen apart. I'd put it this way: if the resurrection didn't happen, then I have no confidence in the Gospel at all and it is just not worth believing.

Resurrection changes everything

If the cross is God's "No!" to sin, then the resurrection is His magnificent life-giving "Yes!" to hope and transformation. Indeed, despite the fact that the resurrection is often relegated to a few lines in a sermon about the cross, the reality is that the whole of the book of Acts is dependent upon the bold and hope-giving proclamation of the *resurrected* Christ,

144

and the epistles of the New Testament would make almost no sense if the resurrection did not sit at the centre of the Church's convictions about Jesus.

In short, the resurrection changes everything.

> The Epistles depend entirely on the assumption that Jesus is a living, reigning Saviour who is now the exalted head of the church, who is to be trusted, worshipped and adored and who will some day return in power and great glory to reign as King over the earth.
>
> Wayne Grudem, *Systematic Theology*

The conviction that Jesus Christ rose from the dead three days after His cold and lifeless corpse was placed in a borrowed tomb is the lynchpin of Christian faith. Without it, His life, His death, and His words do not make sense. If He did not rise from the dead, then His teaching was a lie, His conversations were misleading at best and downright cruel at worst, and His whole ministry becomes meaningless. The apostle Paul argued that if Christ did not rise from the dead, we would be the most miserable (and I would suggest most misled) people on Planet Earth.

The resurrection of Jesus Christ lay at the heart of Paul's understanding of his faith. There is no way of comprehending the Kingdom of God, the power of forgiveness, life after death, hope, transformation or anything else within New Testament faith without the resurrection sitting at the heart of the story.

Indeed, the life of Jesus without the resurrection of Jesus would be a wonderful moral example, but it would not fundamentally give us hope. The death of Jesus without the resurrection of Jesus would not lift our fear of death and it would not give us the assurance that our sin was destroyed for ever. And it goes without saying that the life of the Spirit, the intercessory ministry of Jesus now, and His promised return would be meaningless and impossible if He had not risen from the dead.

Thomas Merton, a Trappist monk, once said that it is of the very essence of Christianity to face suffering and death, not because they are good, not because they have meaning, but because the resurrection of Jesus has robbed them of their meaning.

Just how powerful is the "transforming power" of God the Son?

The resurrection of Jesus does not simply affect us as individuals, though it certainly does that, but it also changes the future of the entire planet. It is the first sign of the ushering in of a brand-new Kingdom that will never end. Indeed, Paul tells us that the whole Creation "groans and yearns" for the power of the resurrected Christ to transform it.

The apostle John paints the resurrection story as a new Creation story in his Gospel. Remember that Creation begins in a "garden" in Genesis 1 and the New Creation will be consummated when the world becomes a Garden City, according to the imagery of the book of Revelation (also written by John). It is surely not a coincidence, therefore, that in John 20 we see resurrection taking place in a garden and Jesus appearing to Mary as a gardener!

The implications of John's account are clear. It is in the moment of resurrection that life springs out of death and light springs out of darkness. This is the moment the world has been waiting for. That is why all the epistles and the entire understanding of the New Testament concept of hope and life and victory rest on resurrection. It is because in resurrection we see the absolute power of Jesus Christ to save, rescue, and transform us, our culture, and the very ground on which we stand – the planet on which we live. There are three key areas we can briefly explore to help us understand the power of the transformation that the resurrection of Jesus displays:

- It transforms people.
- It transforms the planet.
- It transforms our purpose.

There are also three key ways in which resurrection brings transformation:

- It conquers Satan and evil.
- It removes the fear of death.
- It instils a new sense of hope and "re-creation".

The fact that Jesus rose from the dead gives us this unbreakable assurance that God wins, and that changes everything.

It doesn't make sense that someone could be born of a

virgin, die, and then rise again. It doesn't make sense that they can ascend into heaven and then return. It doesn't make sense to follow a man who died almost 2,000 years ago. It doesn't make sense – unless, of course, it is true.

I can't make you believe, and God certainly won't force you to follow Him. He gives us a choice. He allows us to decide. That's unbelievable too, I think.

Eugene Peterson, in his book *The Jesus Way: A Conversation on the Ways That Jesus Is the Way*, says:

> The way of Jesus cannot be imposed or mapped – it requires an active participation in following Jesus as he leads us through sometimes strange and unfamiliar territory, in circumstances that become clear only in the hesitations and questionings, in the pauses and reflections where we engage in prayerful conversation with one another and with him.
>
> Eugene H. Peterson, *The Jesus Way: A Conversation on the Ways That Jesus Is the Way*

Having confidence in Jesus doesn't mean that life is always easy. There are many times when the road seems vague and the way seems dark. Yet Jesus is reliable. He never lets go of us. He just asks us to trust Him. To take Him at His word. To believe that what He said about Himself is true.

It is unbelievable to me that God would be willing to go to such lengths to demonstrate His love for us. It's unbelievable to me that Jesus' life and message are still changing millions of lives. It is unbelievable to me that the grace and mercy and power of God might only be a moment away from you as you read these words.

I don't know how this all works, but I know that it does.

As I am writing these words, we are in the season of Advent, a time when we remember who Jesus is and why He came. I don't get it. But, my God, I believe it.

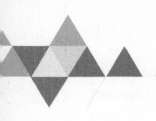

Chapter Seven

Unstoppable:
I believe in the Holy Spirit...

I believe in the Holy Spirit,
the holy catholic Church,
the communion of saints,
the forgiveness of sins,
the resurrection of the body,
and the life everlasting.

In the beginning, when God created the heavens and the
earth, the earth was a formless void and darkness covered
the face of the deep, while a wind from God swept over the
face of the waters. Then God said, "Let there be light"; and
there was light.

The opening words of the Jewish and Christian Scriptures
Genesis 1:1–4

The Spirit and the bride say, "Come."
And let everyone who hears say, "Come."
And let everyone who is thirsty come.
Let anyone who wishes take the water of life as a gift.

Some of the closing words of the Christian Scriptures
Revelation 22:17

If I asked you to draw the Holy Spirit, what would you
draw? Would you draw a fire, a dove or a wind? Would

you draw water or would you draw oil? Would you draw a mist or would you draw a person? It's not an easy question to answer, is it? That's partly because the Holy Spirit is not an easy part of the Trinity to get your head around. I guess it is partly because the Holy Spirit is a bit of a mysterious figure. As we will explore in this chapter, the Spirit points to the Father and to the Son and away from Himself. Should I have said "Herself", do you think? Or maybe "Itself" would be better? I have a view on using the pronoun "Him" for the Holy Spirit, by the way; I am just trying to show that there is actually quite a lot of controversy concerning this particular part of the historical Christian faith. It is interesting that such division exists over the role and function of the Spirit in the life of the Church, when after all one of His central roles is to unite us and enable us to recognize (according to the apostle Paul in his letters to the Churches in Ephesus and Corinth) that we are one body with different functions, and that, although we might look, sound, and even behave differently, there really is only one Holy Spirit.

He, She, It, What?

Let me start by trying to explain the language and pronoun question. There are some theologians and Bible teachers who feel comfortable referring to the Holy Spirit as either "she" or "it". While I appreciate the reasons for this, I struggle with it. The reason for using the female pronoun is predominantly the connecting of the Spirit with the idea or concept of wisdom that is found in Proverbs 8. The Greek word for wisdom, in that context, is plural. There are a number of reasons why I am uncomfortable with that. The first is that the idea of wisdom in Proverbs is not exactly the same as the idea of the Holy Spirit. Furthermore, if there is a connection between wisdom in Proverbs and any part of the Trinity, it is far more likely to be a connection with the Son of God, who is described in John 1 as the *Logos*. *Logos* is a closer parallel to wisdom, although they are still not the same (or compare the use of *sophia* and the use of Christ in 1 Corinthians).

More importantly for me, though, there is no evidence in the Bible of the Holy Spirit being given a female pronoun. I accept and celebrate that God is above gender and that we must be careful not to give the impression that God is a man, when He clearly isn't. That having been said, I prefer to use the pronoun predominantly used in the New Testament to refer to the Holy Spirit, and that is definitely "He". Occasionally the pronoun "it" is used when referencing the idea of breath or wind (such as in John 3), but it is very clear that the Spirit is almost entirely referred to as "He" in the New Testament. So in this chapter I will use the pronoun "He", but that does not mean I am suggesting that the Spirit is a man.

The Creed and the Spirit

This last section of the Apostles' Creed is the one that contains most of the controversial statements for today's Churches. There are sections of it that seem to divide the

Roman Catholic Church, the Protestant Churches, and the Orthodox Church. The last section of the Creed states:

> I believe in the Holy Spirit,
> the holy catholic Church,
> the communion of saints,
> the forgiveness of sins,
> the resurrection of the body,
> and the life everlasting.

On reading it, some people think that it is "light" on the Holy Spirit. After all, there is only one line in there about the Holy Spirit, right? Wrong. Actually the whole section from "I believe in the Holy Spirit" through to the end of the Creed is explaining some of the aspects and ministry of the Holy Spirit. It's a mistake to read just the top line as being concerned with the Holy Spirit. The statement connects belief in the Holy Spirit to the rest of the lines. In other words, it is a belief in the Holy Spirit and His ministry and power that leads to a belief in:

• the holy catholic Church
• the communion of the saints
• the forgiveness of sins
• the resurrection of the body
• and the life everlasting.

To put it another way, without the Holy Spirit's presence and ministry among us, the breath of life that connects the Church across the world and down the ages would not be present. If He were not present in all places there would be no sense of communion and unity among us. It is the Spirit who makes the forgiveness of God real in our lives and who helps us not just to believe it but to experience it. The Spirit is the one who raised Christ from the dead, and He is the same Spirit who will raise us from the dead and give us new life in every sense. And it is the Holy Spirit who Himself gives us the life that will never end – everlasting life. Without Him, the whole Creed actually becomes meaningless, because, without Him, the Christian life is impossible.

We cannot function properly without the Holy Spirit

The reality is that we cannot lead a Christian life without the power and presence of the Holy Spirit working in us and through us. We can't understand the Bible without His help, we aren't aware of sin without His help, we aren't able to worship, praise, and serve God properly without His help, and we can't grow in maturity and character without His being at work in our lives. In short, it is impossible to live for Christ at all without Him. Yet so many people try to. I often think about the fact that the Holy Spirit departed from the Temple in Israel (the story is told in Ezekiel chapters 8 – 11), and I wonder what was worse. Was the worse thing that He departed, or was the worse thing that everything carried on for another six years without anyone noticing? I find myself wondering how many Churches and ministries continue to function without any sense of the Spirit's power or presence in their lives and their work. That's a scary thought. Would I notice if the Spirit stopped anointing me? That's even scarier.

Gordon Fee is one of the world's leading Pentecostal theologians, in my view. In his magnum opus, *God's Empowering Presence*, Fee says this about the person and work of the Holy Spirit:

> The crucial role of the Spirit in Paul's life... as the dynamic, experiential reality of Christian life – is often either overlooked or given mere lip service... I am equally convinced that the Spirit in Paul's experience and theology was always thought of in terms of the personal presence of God. The Spirit is God's way of being present, powerfully present, in our lives and communities as we await the consummation of the kingdom of God. Precisely because he understood the Spirit as God's personal presence, Paul also understood the Spirit always in terms of an empowering presence; whatever else, for Paul the Spirit was an experienced reality.
>
> Gordon Fee, *God's Empowering Presence: The Holy Spirit in the Letters of Paul*

"Whatever else, for Paul the Spirit was an experienced reality." That strikes me as one of the most challenging lines I have offered in this book so far. It links so closely to the idea of confidence, doesn't it? Without the experienced reality of the Spirit in our lives it could be said that all else is window dressing. As we explore the purpose and the role of the Holy Spirit, we will see the absolute centrality of His ministry if we are to stand before God – or the world – with any level of confidence.

Trying to function without the power of the Spirit in our lives is like trying to breathe without lungs. He is so intrinsically vital that there is actually no way in which the Christian life can be lived properly without His presence and power being at work. Let's leave aside, for a moment, whether you and I agree on whether all of the "gifts" of the Spirit are available today or whether some of them died out with the end of the apostolic era. A cursory reading of Ephesians and Romans tells us that, without the Spirit's presence and work in our lives, we are sunk:

> In him you also, when you had heard the word of truth, the gospel of your salvation, and had believed in him, were marked with the seal of the promised Holy Spirit; this is the pledge of our inheritance towards redemption as God's own people, to the praise of his glory.
>
> Ephesians 1:13–14

> But you are not in the flesh; you are in the Spirit, since the Spirit of God dwells in you. Anyone who does not have the Spirit of Christ does not belong to him. But if Christ is in you, though the body is dead because of sin, the Spirit is life because of righteousness. If the Spirit of him who raised Jesus from the dead dwells in you, he who raised Christ

from the dead will give life to your mortal bodies
also through his Spirit that dwells in you.

Romans 8:9–11

Paul tells the Christians in Galatia to keep in step with the Spirit (Galatians 5). He tells the Ephesians to be continually refreshed and filled with the Spirit, the implication being they need His spiritual life as much as they need to breathe (Ephesians 5). He tells the Corinthians about the central role of the Spirit in producing gifts and giving them wisdom and guidance. He urges the Church in Thessalonica not to quench the Spirit. Throughout his letters, the Spirit is his constant refrain. Paul drives home again and again that if followers of Christ want to keep following, then they need the ongoing, consistent, daily, and continual power of the Holy Spirit in their lives.

We still do.

What does the Bible have to say about the Holy Spirit?

The Spirit has many names and is seen in many metaphors and forms throughout the course of the Scriptures:

- The Spirit of Life (Ezekiel 37:1–10; John 6:63; Romans 8:2)
- The Spirit of the Jehovah (Isaiah 11:2; 61:1–3)
- The Spirit of Holiness (Romans 1:4)
- The Oil of Gladness (Hebrews 1:9)
- The Holy Spirit of Promise (Genesis 2:7; Luke 11:13; John 20:22; Ephesians 1:13)

- The Spirit of Jesus Christ (Acts 16:6–7; Romans 8:9; 1 Corinthians 3:16; Philippians 1:19)
- The Spirit of the Living God (1 Corinthians 3:16; 2 Corinthians 3:6)
- The Lord (Acts 28:25; Hebrews 3:7)
- The Spirit of Flame or Fire (Isaiah 4:3–4; Matthew 3:11)
- The Spirit of Judgment (Isaiah 4:4)
- The Spirit of His Son (Galatians 4:6)
- The Spirit of Glory (1 Peter 4:14)
- God (Acts 5:3–4)
- The Eternal Spirit (Hebrews 9:14)
- The Spirit of Grace (Hebrews 10:29)
- The Spirit of Wisdom and Knowledge (Isaiah 11:2)
- The Spirit of Knowledge and the Fear of the Lord (Isaiah 11:2)
- The Spirit of Compassion and Supplication (Zechariah 12:10)
- The Comforter / Advocate (John 14:26)
- The Spirit of Truth (John 14:17; 15:26)
- The Spirit of Counsel and Might (Acts 1:8; 8:29; 16:6–7).

In fact, in the first few verses of Genesis we read that the Spirit was present and active in creation (Genesis 1:1–2).

From that moment of intimate involvement in Creation, we see the Spirit directly connected with life throughout the Scriptures. As God "speaks" through the Creation narratives, so it is the wind or the "breath" of the Spirit that carries His words.

In the building of the Tabernacle and the Temple, it is

the Spirit who enables and empowers various people to perform their tasks. From Bezalel and Oholiab (see Exodus 31) to the prophets and the seers, the Holy Spirit was empowering and intimately engaging in lives throughout the Old Testament narrative.

In Genesis 6 we read of God's sober warning that His Spirit will not always strive with people. As one reads the pages of the Old Testament and follows the longings and yearnings of Israel, one sees a God who is nudging His people forward. Noah was guided by a dove (a symbol of the Holy Spirit); God spoke to Moses through a burning bush (fire being a symbol of the Spirit); when they were thirsty, God provided the Israelites with water (a symbol of the Holy Spirit); God led the Israelites with fire and cloud (both symbols of the Spirit); when the kings of Israel were anointed, they were anointed with oil (a symbol of the Holy Spirit) and so the images and metaphors go on. The Holy Spirit can be seen and heard throughout the story of Israel.

Yet something happens as you journey through the Scriptures. Throughout the Old Testament there is also an ever-increasing sense of promise that the Spirit will be even more intimately connected to and involved with the lives of God's people. God promises the people of Israel that He will take the Law, which had been written on stones, and write it "on their hearts" (see Jeremiah 31:33) and He promises that He will take away their heart of "stone" and replace it with a heart of "flesh" (see Ezekiel 36:26). Through the prophet Joel He promises that there will be a day when He will "pour out His Spirit on all flesh" (see Joel 2) and He will give gifts to His people – special gifts such as visions and dreams and prophecy. The Old Testament closes with a yearning for this gift, a reaching out for this intimacy with God and His involvement in the lives of His people.

The New Testament

The New Testament opens with a flurry of Holy Spirit activity. This is seen particularly in the account of the births of both John the Baptist and Jesus in the Gospel of Luke (see chapters 1–3). The Spirit is the force by which Mary conceives (1:35). The Spirit touches John the Baptist while he grows in Elizabeth's womb when the young Mary goes to see her cousin (1:41). The Spirit causes both Anna and Simeon to prophesy (2:25–39). It is the Holy Spirit that empowers Jesus and rests on Him at His baptism (3:21–23). It is the Spirit that forces Jesus into the wilderness to be tempted (4:1). It is the Spirit that rests on Him when He announces His manifesto in the Nazareth synagogue (4:16ff.). The ministry of Jesus could not be understood without the intimacy and involvement of the Spirit.

When Jesus talks to Nicodemus (John 3), He explains that the Holy Spirit is an untameable wind (3:8), yet without Him conversion is not possible and life in God is inaccessible (3:3, 7). As Jesus prepares His disciples for the crucifixion, He talks to them about the centrality, the importance, and the work of the Holy Spirit (John 14–17). The Lord Jesus tells His disciples that the Spirit will guide them into all truth; He will convict them of sin, or righteousness, and of judgment to come. He will defend them against the attacks of the enemy. He will empower them and nurture them. Yet He will also comfort them and give them assurance.

The early years of the Church

After the resurrection of Jesus, He meets His disciples in Jerusalem and tells them that they are to wait there until they are empowered "from on high" (Acts 1:4, 8); then, on the Day of Pentecost, the Holy Spirit is poured out on the Church and the prophecy of Joel is fulfilled (Acts 2; Joel 2). God is now indwelling His people by the power of the Holy Spirit. He is no longer resting on them temporarily; He is resident within them. And with that residency come both gifts of the Spirit (1 Corinthians 12; Romans 12; Ephesians 4, etc.) and the fruit of the Spirit, which is evidence of increasingly Christlike character and attitudes (Galatians 5). The Church in the New Testament is carried along by the wind of the Spirit, often trying to keep up with Him as He pushes the Gospel of Jesus Christ out into the world. The New Testament closes with an invitation from the Holy Spirit to come and drink from His well and to meet the risen Christ (Revelation 22).

The Holy Spirit continues to push the Church today. He continues to give gifts to God's people, to push us into new areas, to challenge us to think differently, to empower us for witnessing to Christ. He continues to shape the Church and to defend us from the enemy. As Paul warned the Ephesians, so we too must learn to fight our battles with spiritual weapons and to recognize that we face a dangerous foe (Ephesians 6).

We are as dependent on Him now as we have always been. Without Him, our faith becomes dry and lifeless, like the valley of dry bones in the vision of Ezekiel (chapter 37), but, with Him, we can advance the Kingdom of God and further the purposes of Christ.

The Spirit gives us confidence

The Holy Spirit gives God's people confidence. He reminds us that we are loved and held by God and He empowers us to serve God. Paul's words to the believers in Rome are a powerful reminder of the place and power of the Spirit, not just in their personal lives and their understanding of themselves before God but also in their understanding of what God is doing throughout the world and in the very Creation.

It is the Spirit who enables the Christian to come with confidence, boldness, and intimacy before God. It is the Spirit that enables us to understand God as our Father and Jesus as our Lord. It is the Spirit that empowers us to live for God, to face challenge and ridicule, and, if need be, to die for Christ. It is the Spirit who fashions character in us. It is the Spirit who gives us the gifts and talents that we need to accomplish God's purposes. It is the Spirit who illuminates God's word to us and brings revelation to our hearts.

Yet it is also the Spirit who is at work in the world, groaning with the Creation as the very planet yearns for the deliverance that will come in the ultimate salvation of Christ. It is the Spirit that pushes us and prompts us and challenges us to stand up against injustice, to make a difference in the world, to speak out on behalf of those who cannot speak out for themselves. The Spirit drives the Church from Jerusalem in Acts 1 to Rome in Acts 28. He is always one step ahead of the body of Christ, prompting us to break new ground, calling us to step into new territory, painting on a bigger canvas, and calling us to a bigger vision.

He is always speaking to us; the question is whether or not we are listening.

What is the Spirit saying to the Church?

Let anyone who has an ear listen to what the Spirit is saying to the churches.

Revelation 2:7, 11, 17, 29; 3:6, 13, 22

Every generation of the Church must think through what God might be saying to us and how we can respond to His leading and to His guiding. Not only should each generation do that, but the body of Christ must also do it regularly. As the culture shifts around us, we must re-examine what Christ is truly saying to us and commit ourselves again to being faithful in our witness for Him – in our actions, our attitudes, our thinking, and our conversations. That rigorous commitment to reflection and listening to the voice of the Spirit must happen not only in local Churches but in "the body" in a community, a neighbourhood, a district, a nation, and in whatever bonds of fellowship and relationship we have entered into with other believers.

Beyond labels but getting to the core: Returning to the concept of one Church, without compromising on the truth

I have no desire to perpetuate the unhelpful differentiation that takes place between Christians with arguments about whether we describe ourselves as "evangelical" or "protestant" or "catholic" or "reformed" or "progressive" or "Pentecostal" or "charismatic" or "liberal", etc. It strikes me that we need a new-found confidence in the "holy catholic Church". Don't misunderstand what I am saying. There are many aspects of the doctrines and practices of denominations that I would find difficult. I don't think unity at any cost is an ideal towards which we should strive. I am talking about a new, Spirit-forged unity of mission and purpose across the true body of Christ, which is made up of all men and women who love and honour Jesus and call on Him as Lord.

I think many of the labels we use to describe one another end up being unhelpful and become like the emperor's new clothes if we are not careful. We can end up missing our own nakedness and nonsense because we have bought into the latest definition of what it means to be compassionate or culturally sensitive. We believe the lies that the labels bring with them and proudly define ourselves by wrong or faulty descriptions, and we are too proud to see that the labels are actually non-existent fabrics and that the only thing we are revealing is our own prejudices.

I think the far more important question is whether we

are in line with what the Bible describes as Christian. That descriptor alone is the one that I think we will have to allow to define us, confine us, refine us, and ultimately align us. I will pick up on this point of view later.

Of course many people use the idea of being "biblical" as nothing more than a justification for their own prejudices and preconceptions. I want to avoid that too. What I mean by being "biblical" is whether or not we are obeying the overarching and clear teaching of the Scriptures and living within its parameters.

God speaks today to His Son's bride through His word by His Spirit

The phrase "Let anyone who has an ear listen to what the Spirit is saying to the churches" is repeated seven times in the revelation of Jesus Christ given to John the apostle on the island of Patmos. It is in Revelation 2:7, 11, 17, 29; 3:6, 13, 22.

Depending on why you think the revelation of Christ was given to John, these words will have different implications prophetically. However, they have a clear meaning for each of the believing communities that initially received them. The implication is that God has something to say to each believing community in the light of its own witness, its culture, the pressures it faces, and the things it believes and practises.

I think every single Church or group of Churches must ask this same fundamental question and allow the answer to shape the Church's witness to the wider culture and context:

What is the Spirit saying to the Church?

The pattern of question and answer in Revelation

- Jesus describes Himself to them in terms from chapter 1 of Revelation.
- He is aware of what each Church is really like – both positive (excluding Sardis and Laodicea) and negative (excluding Smyrna and Philadelphia).
- Having addressed the reality of their state, Jesus gives them comfort and encouragement and challenges and commandments.
- Each Church is told to listen carefully to what the Holy Spirit is saying.
- A blessing is promised to those who "overcome".

If we examine what the Spirit is saying to the Churches in Revelation, we will see that each of the contexts speaks somehow into our context too. Christ would have us understand something of who He really is. He knows exactly what we are like as a Church in the nation and in our own cities and denominations and networks. He wants to comfort and strengthen us where we are getting it right and challenge, confront, and command us to change where we are getting it wrong. He gives our Churches the freedom to respond to Him and He makes us promises and gives us warnings concerning what we do in the light of what He is saying to us.

What was the Spirit saying to the Churches in Asia Minor?

Ephesus (2:1–7):

Commended for the fact that they are holding to doctrinal truth and being sure to stay in the truth, but challenged because they have lost their first love. They are told to remember, repent, and do the things that they did at first. If they don't, their "lampstand" will be removed. If they do, they will be given the tree of paradise to eat from.

Application:

We may hold to the truth but we may at the same time lose our passion and intimacy. If we don't fix that, then we will lose our place in our culture and society. If we do fix it, then ultimately we will be nourished and sustained.

Smyrna (2:8–11):

They are standing in the midst of persecution and they are encouraged to be faithful to the end, when they will be given the crown of life and they will not endure the pain of the second death.

Application:

If we stand firm in the face of opposition and challenge and remain faithful in the midst of that challenge, then we will be honoured by Christ for our commitment to Him and ultimately kept safe from a far worse fate than rejection by society.

Pergamum (2:12-17):

They have held fast to the name of Christ and not denied their faith, but they have allowed false teaching to infiltrate their ranks and their thinking. If they don't repent, then Christ Himself will oppose them, but if they do repent, they will be nourished and provided for miraculously and they will be given a stone with a new name on it.

Application:

If we claim to live under the identity of belonging to Christ, then our words and beliefs must reflect His commands and not the commands or ideas of our culture. If we fail to guard our consistency, Christ Himself will oppose us. If we remain faithful and authentic, God will ensure that we are provided for and will continually reveal our new identity and purpose "in Him" to us.

Thyatira (2:18-19):

Their growing love and compassion is evidenced in their love and care and service, but they are increasingly lacking any sense of correct evaluation and discernment of their culture and its messages and they increasingly tolerate heresy without challenging it. The solution is to hold true, and stay committed to Christ and who He is and to His message without wavering. If they don't do that, then God will give them exactly what they want – the consequences of their own actions will be worked out upon them. If they do commit themselves to faithful ministry and service, they will shine brightly like the morning star and they will have authority over the nations.

Application:

We should continue to be committed to the service of those who are broken and need to experience God's grace and love in and through us (though not at the expense of truth and faithfulness to the Gospel), and to keeping the Gospel unchanged in our hearts and communities of faith. If we fail to hold true to Christ then we will become what we seem to want to be – no more than an additional social service and one voice among many kindly voices. We may gain political clout but we will lose all spiritual authority. If we remain true to Christ, we will become clearer, brighter, and stronger in our witness, and our authority among the nations will increase.

Sardis (3:1–6):

There are a few people in this Church who remain faithful and true to the purposes of Christ yet are engaged in a works-based, self-justifying series of deeds that are dead. They should remain true to Scripture and turn from their wrong sense of self-justification. If they don't, then they will face the sudden and unexpected judgment of God through Christ, but if they do, they will be clothed in new white garments and their names will never be removed from the Lamb's book of life and will be openly confessed before God and the angelic powers.

Application:

God has some who are remaining faithful in His Church, but we must not seek to build our identity, our purpose, and our raison d'être on the wrong foundations of works and self-justification. We must remain true to what Christ has said and turn away from our false security and pride. If we don't then we will be caught off guard by God's judgment and we will be ill prepared for what He does. If we do, we will have a fresh sense of our identity, purpose, and security in Christ and we will know the blessing of God's continual approval of us and our ministry.

Philadelphia (3:7–13):

They are patiently standing strong in the midst of all that is happening around them and they refuse to deny who God is or what He says. They are called to remain true and not lose sight of what they have "in Christ". If they do remain true, they will be made "pillars" in God's Temple and be inscribed with new names of God Himself, the New Jerusalem, and Christ.

Application:

As we stand strong in the midst of cultural, political, and social pressures, we will be strengthened by God Himself and we will have a deep and intuitive sense of God's identity being part of who we are and the attributes and values of the Kingdom (heaven) being part of our DNA, and a special and increasing sense of Christ "in us" as our power and strength.

Laodicea (3:14–22):

They are spiritually blind, spiritually bankrupt, and spiritually naked, and as a result they are lukewarm. Therefore Christ will spit them out of His mouth because they are neither one thing nor another. If they repent and return to the undiluted truth of who Christ is and what He has for them, then He will renew His fellowship with them and they will reign with Him.

Application:

Where we think we are clear and focused, wealthy, and at ease and decked with kudos and admirable characteristics, if we have lost our zeal, diluted our commitment, and squeezed ourselves into our culture, then we are actually a parody of what we think we are because we have no sense of direction and nothing of worth to share with others, and we are ultimately embarrassing ourselves by the starkness of our brazenness. The only way out of this is to return to who Christ is and ask for His mercy. Otherwise, we will be expelled from our culture and find ourselves unpalatable to Christ. We won't fit in anywhere and will therefore be rejected.

What is the Spirit saying to us?

- **The lesson of Ephesus:** We need a fresh encounter with the Holy Spirit and we need to ask God to make us individuals and communities of authenticity who match our love for truth with our desire for intimacy with Christ and engagement with society.

171

- **The lesson of Smyrna:** In the face of opposition, we must remain true to the person and work of Jesus. Opposition is increasing in the UK and the USA, culturally, religiously, politically, socially, and economically. Faith is encountering increased levels of attack, undermining, and persecution across the Middle East, in South-East Asia, and in Africa. This persecution is growing, and we must find ways not just of standing up for ourselves but of standing with our brothers and sisters.

- **The lesson of Pergamum:** We must also stand for truth among ourselves. We are seeing an increase in departures from the classic definitions of matters such as biblical authority, the person and work of Christ, what it means to be a disciple, what we believe about the nature and function of the Church, the purpose and centrality of proclamation, mission, and worship, and the plain, clear instructions of Scripture with regard to faithfulness, sexual purity, ethical behaviour, moral uprightness, and definitions of absolute truth. Just as in the days of the Early Church, these departures from both orthodoxy and orthopraxy represent a serious threat to the future witness of the Church and to its effectiveness. We must discover what it means to live consistently under the authority of God's revealed will and purposes. He will sustain us, but we must be willing to be obedient. We have a biblical and familial responsibility to challenge those who claim to be Christian but then deny Christ's clear teaching and instruction, even if it makes us unpopular. Faithfulness is more important than popularity.

- **The lesson of Thyatira:** We are undoubtedly called to engage in the love, service, and support of those who are marginalized and on the edge of society. We must offer ourselves wholeheartedly to the mission of God in the world and in our communities, but we must not allow this to lead to a loss of our theologically and biblically shaped identity and purpose. The great challenge to the Church in Europe and North America is that we are allowing ourselves to be defined by the wider culture's definition of "Christian" and we are lacking insight and clarity over what is right and what is wrong. We are becoming enmeshed in arguments that are driven by a lack of discernment. The voices of our culture, our politicians, and our communities are too loud if they are drowning out the voice of the Spirit. We are failing to challenge the culture and instead we are in danger of changing the Gospel to fit in with it. For fear of being labelled, attacked or excluded, we are rushing to affirm the values of our society socially, sexually, politically, and economically instead of being the faithful witnesses to Christ that we are called to be. We are in danger of becoming a subcultural social-activist lobby instead of a counter-cultural movement for spiritual and societal transformation.

- **The lesson of Sardis:** We are allowing a self-selecting band of mutually justifying leading figures within the Church to move the baseline of what it means to be authentically Christian. One after the other, we are seeing leaders redefine what it means to be biblical and Christlike in the light of one another's theological positions. The result is an ever-increasing circle of mutually supportive positions that are actually moving Churches away from historical positions of faithfulness and obedience. We see this sense of mutual affirmation and perpetual self validation in the stands of denominations or leading figures within the justice and peace or social action wings of the Church. We see it in the increasing clamour for political and societal endorsement and in the increasing attempts by Churches to justify their positions by the positions of other Churches or church leaders. We need to return to a sense of Christ-centredness and work out what biblical faithfulness looks like based on the actual text, not on a Marcion-like reduction of it.

- **The lesson of Philadelphia:** Alongside all the challenges to depart from the truth there are increased and powerful calls for a return to what it means to be "in Christ". The last twenty years have seen a plethora of resources, teaching, preaching, and passion for rediscovering our identity "in Christ", our purpose "in Christ" and our destiny "in Christ". These are evidence of a deep and powerful movement of the Holy Spirit in the midst of the challenges of our culture and our context. They also display the deepening yearning in the lives of men and women outside our Churches and in our communities who want to know what "authenticity" and real life and true purpose look like. God is with those Churches and Christians who are seeking to uncover, celebrate, and enable a deeper understanding of the Church's and the individual Christian's identity in Jesus. This should be at the heart of our attempts to disciple, empower, and equip God's people.

- **The lesson of Laodicea:** God is free to lift His continued anointing from a Church or groups of Churches that do not do His will. If we continue in persistent arrogance and pride, we will find our effectiveness destroyed, our identity decimated, and our purpose lost. There are Churches and perhaps whole denominations and movements that are celebrating their heritage but which have lost their way. They have become so caught up in guarding what they once were that they have lost sight of what they are called to be. God will not allow this situation to continue and we will see a stronger, more vibrant, and spiritually alive Church emerging **at the same time** as the lifeless religious institutions of traditionalism are collapsing and dying. This provides us with an opportunity to repent of what we think has defined us as successful, to reject any label that we have thought of as more important than the word "Christian" or "follower of Jesus", and to discover fresh confidence, power, and renewal in the presence of the Holy Spirit, the call to obedience and surrender, and the truth of who God is as displayed in Scripture.

Do we have the confidence to respond?

We find ourselves in the most exciting generation of the Church, with several things happening at the same time.

- Opposition to us is increasing and dilution of the Gospel and its central truths is proliferating.
- Religious traditionalism and unbiblical division are being drained of life and are in their death throes.
- Spiritual laxity and pride are both being exposed.
- Genuine longing for authenticity is increasing.
- The determination of some to stand up for Christ and to be true to His word is growing.
- A battle is raging over whether we will be defined by our culture or by the Bible and the person and work of Christ.

Response 1 – Openness, Commitment, Humility

If we respond with humility, openness, and a renewed commitment to work with others who are followers of Christ and are seeking to live under the authority of God's word, God's Spirit, and God's Son, then we will see new networks, new partnerships, and new life emerging from our current context and we will have greater effectiveness in our witness and we will see awakening and renewal.

Response 2 – Pride, Arrogance, Cultural congruity

If we respond with pride, arrogance, or a desire to "fit into" our culture with its demands and confining expectations of the Church, we will lose our anointing and become an irrelevant voice in our nation for one of two reasons. Either we are saying only what society wants to hear and therefore we are saying nothing, or we are so detached from our culture that we are speaking a language they don't understand and answering questions they are not asking.

The response we make will determine the path we walk.

Unstoppable

I came to faith in a Pentecostal Church. I am still part of the Elim Church movement, and proud to be ordained by them. I lead Gold Hill, a member of the family of the Baptist Union and, like many other churches across the world, a Church that has a heart for God's world and an openness to the Holy Spirit. During my ministry I have been blessed by working with every denomination in the UK. I count it a privilege to have learned a great deal from each one. I have seen the beauty of God's Church. I've also seen the ugliness that the Church can have.

The pain of division.

The dangers of jealousy and fear.

The ugliness of personal agendas.

What happens when a Church loses sight of its core purpose.

Yet through all my experiences, both good and bad, I have come to believe that the Church is a glorious and beautiful bride, full of hope and possibility. When we remain open to the Holy Spirit and allow Him to move in us and through us, something happens. When God's people allow His Spirit to breathe fresh life into us, anything becomes possible. Mountains move. Lives change. Hope is born.

The Holy Spirit is at work in the world today. He is drawing people to Christ. He is broadening the vision and deepening the resilience of God's people. Across the UK, Churches, prompted by the Holy Spirit, are getting involved in their communities, making a difference in families, speaking out on the matters of environmental stewardship, human rights, education, housing, and healthcare. Individual Christians are catching a fresh glimpse of God using them in their workplace, their schools, and their streets. The old barriers between the "secular" and the "sacred" are tumbling down. God is on the move.

You see, the Spirit is unstoppable. He is fulfilling His role of uplifting Jesus, infilling the saints, confronting the devil, and transforming lives.

I don't think there has ever been a better time to be a follower of Christ in the United Kingdom. God has called us to a great task, but He has not left us alone to do it. He is with us; He is within us. He is for us and not against us. He has gone ahead of us and He is behind us.

Christ will build His Church and the gates of Hades will not prevail against it.

The Gospel still works.

The Creed still stands.

The call has not changed.

The challenge has been laid.

What we do with it is up to us.

Conclusion

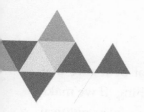

Chapter Eight

An unbelievable task: The call to change the world

Our understanding of God is too small.

And when our understanding of God is too small, our understanding of the Gospel and of mission becomes too small as well.

What a disaster.

The Gospel is the remarkable news that Jesus Christ is Lord and has dealt with our sin and separation. It is the message that God was in Christ reconciling the world to Himself. Every aspect of the life of Jesus speaks of this remarkable message of hope, forgiveness, reconciliation and invitation. The implications of the Gospel are shown in the way we live our lives, the decisions that we make and the priorities that we set. The Gospel sets us free as part of Christ's Church to live out the mission of God in the world. We are brought into Christ's family, the Church, when we believe the simple truth that through the life, death, and resurrection of Christ, our sins are dealt with, our separation is no more, and our purpose has been changed. The Gospel changes everything in our lives and everything in the way we view the world. The Gospel gives us a new mission. If it does not, then we have made our God too small.

Mission is what God calls us to do in the world. We

must be careful not to fall into the trap of believing that "mission" and the "Gospel" are the same thing. If we make that mistake, then we begin to believe that social or political action are in and of themselves the Gospel of Jesus. This can never be true. The call to change the world is a consequence of faith in Christ and obedience to His cause, it is not in and of itself conversion. Conversion is the turning of our lives over to God, trusting in His Son alone for our salvation and our peace with God. As followers of Christ, we then live out the remainder of our lives as His disciples in the world around us fulfilling His mission.

In my last book, *Risk Takers*, I argued that the Gospel was far bigger than just getting people converted. A friend of mine read the book and rang me to tell me, gently but firmly, that I was wrong. He wanted me to know that he believed the Gospel was only about people coming to faith in Jesus; everything else was a *consequence* of that conversion. He helped me to sharpen my thinking and my language.

In the words of the Apostle Paul, we must not be ashamed of the Gospel of Christ (Romans 1:16) and the core message that in Christ, God was reconciling the world to Himself (2 Corinthians 5:19–21). There are many evangelicals who are losing sight of the centrality of conversion. They are replacing the centrality of turning to Christ for forgiveness and reconciliation with being activists in the world and campaigning. I think that is dangerous because you can be a social or political activist, and even be so "in Christ's name", without having experienced His grace and forgiveness in your own life. However, it is impossible to have genuinely experienced His grace and forgiveness in your life without surrendering your life to His purpose and your will to His cause. The mission of God to transform the world flows from the power of the Good News that God was in Christ reconciling the world to Himself. Christ's Lordship is now evidenced in our lives as we join with God in His mission to transform the world.

At the heart of the Good News of Jesus then, we see a God who came to redeem and restore broken people. He did it through the sinless, perfect life of His Son and through the perfect atoning death of that Son on the cross for our sin. Three days later that same Son rose from the dead, conquering death itself. He then taught His disciples about the Kingdom and told them to wait in Jerusalem until they received the power of the Holy Spirit, so that they could be His witnesses in Jerusalem, Judea and to the ends of the earth (Acts 1:4,8). Jesus then ascended to His Father and a few days later He poured out His Holy Spirit upon His disciples so that they could be His witnesses (Acts 2). To be converted leads to us laying down our lives before Christ for His service and His purpose – we become His disciples for the rest of our lives, whether that be short or long. The thief on the cross was converted, then died, so clearly he did not "do" anything else after his conversion. His belief in Christ was enough. It is for us too – but we must be clear that when we confess faith in Christ, our lives are then changed. We become His disciples – we live for Him and not ourselves. We partner with God in His overarching mission, which is the transformation of the world. We do this because we are

183

His disciples, not in order to become His disciples.

Raising the bar – the Good News changes everything

Going to heaven is not the only result of our conversion, as wonderful and beautiful a promise as that is. Nor is it God's purpose simply to fill Churches, though that is also a beautiful thing. God's purpose in sending His Son is to transform the world. Anything less than that vision is simply not good enough. God is at work in this world of ours and He calls us to join Him in the task of transformation. Not just a tinkering around the edges, but a root-and-branch change. Everything changed. Every atom transformed. In the words of George Verwer, the energetic founder of Operation Mobilisation, if your vision doesn't involve changing the world, then it is not big enough.

A simple reading of scripture leaves us in no doubt as to God's purposes. One day, every knee will bow and every tongue will confess that Christ is Lord, to the glory of God the Father (Philippians 2). The whole creation will be changed. The whole world will be transformed as Christ finally and fully establishes His Kingdom (Revelation 21). We, the Church on earth, are now called to live out the mission and purposes of God in the world around us. That involves a call to conversion and a call to discipleship and mission. In Chapter Two, "Anchored, not drowning", I cited some of the core passages that people use to summarize the Good News, before focusing in on 1 Corinthians 15 and the importance of the whole life and ministry of Jesus *according to the Scriptures*. I want to list them again, but this time for a different reason. These verses are "summary" verses for much of what the Gospel is all about:

1. It's about our sin being dealt with and our being rescued (John 3:16)

2. It's about the life and ministry of Jesus (1 Timothy 3:16)

3. It's about the Kingdom (Mark 1:14–15)

4. It's about speaking of and proclaiming the Lordship of Christ (Romans 10:9)

Actually, I want to say that the Gospel is about Jesus and what He has done for us. The purposes and plans of God are so vast and so significant that they incorporate all of these ideas. Jesus' life, death, ministry, message, and ongoing mission are about the establishment of His Kingdom, the assertion of His Lordship, the banishment and defeat of sin and death and hell, the rescuing of a broken and lost world, the transformation of the planet, and the worship of His name. Anything smaller is too small.

We have to learn to raise the bar of our expectations of God. Conversion is not just a decision; it is a step into a whole new way of life. The problem we have with the phrase "Good News" is that the word "good" is overused, and therefore doesn't work. The purposes of God aren't just good, they are *unbelievably* good. They are so good that we just can't catch the meaning.

People I meet are ready for a bigger ask. They are fed up with a small mission and a small understanding of God. They don't want to come to Church to be entertained. They want a vision that is so big that it demands their whole life, their whole future. They want to give their life to something that will make a lasting difference. Too many people are persuaded to give up on their dreams by people who have already given up on theirs. Don't settle for a smaller vision.

As unbelievable as it may sound and as naïve as it may make me look, God, through His Son, Jesus, and the power of the Holy Spirit, is changing the world. One life at a time, one situation at a time, one moment at a time, God is reaching into and across this planet and bringing people out of darkness and into light.

We have to raise the bar. We have to continue to remind people that God is intent on changing *everything*. Not just some things, *everything*. One day His glory will cover the earth as the waters cover the sea. One day *every* knee will bow and *every* tongue will confess that Jesus is Lord. In the meantime, God calls us to live in the tension of the reality of His reign in a broken world. There is not one part of this planet where God's power to change and transform is not present. The ongoing impact of Jesus' life, death, and resurrection on His followers puts Him at the centre of their lives and should be felt in the fields of politics, society, the environment, relationships, spirituality, emotions, economics, psychology, and philosophy, to name just a few.

As unbelievable as it may sound, the bigger we let the mision of God become, the less sceptical the world around us will be. Maybe it is because we have privatized our faith and trivialized our message that the world is so sceptical of us. Maybe, if we started to join the dots, the world around us would get the picture. The Gospel changes the world by changing individuals who then give themselves to God's purposes for His creation. It's God's call on every Christian to live for Him – and He can change the world at every level through His people.

Making disciples, not just making a difference: The power of Christian discipleship

We are not called just to make a difference or even just to make converts, as wonderful as that is. We are called to make disciples and we should not underestimate the power of discipleship.

If we teach people to make a difference, then we are focusing on the task but not on the big picture. You see, you can make a difference without making a disciple, but it is absolutely impossible to make disciples without also making a difference. Disciple a teacher and you'll change a generation of students. Disciple a banker and you will change the culture of the bank. Disciple a politician and you will plant a seed of radical transformation in politics. Disciple a nurse and you will help him or her to be the hands and feet of Jesus all the time.

If we help people to become confident in who God is and what God wants, and we encourage them to see God at work through them everywhere they are and in everything they do, we really will change the world. We spend far too much time encouraging people to do something that is nice and not nearly enough time encouraging people to do what God has called them to do. Why didn't Jesus build a school, a hospital or a hostel? Why didn't the Early Church abandon preaching and teaching and just do nice things? Because they understood that when you made a disciple you were fashioning someone who would take it as *part of their call to follow Christ* to lay down their lives for Him. A disciple commits to seeking to doing good always and to engaging in the challenges and the pain around them whilst pointing to the Saviour of the world. The Early Church focused on making disciples because they that making disciples is the most effective way of changing the world. Disciples lay down every aspect of their lives to the service and purpose of God in mission. Disciples of Jesus don't just seek to make people happy, disciples of Jesus seek to change the world by honouring and serving God with everything they have and everything they are.

Christian discipleship turns the world upside down. It did in the book of Acts and it does today. The disciple understands that in every situation they are to serve God. They get that whatever God asks for, they give Him. That is the unbelievable power of discipleship. It is also why I am a pastor. I am doing what I consider to be the most influential and impactful thing I can do with my life, my gifts, and my skills. Disciples look at their lives and give them to God. They seek to discover what the best use of their time and skills and experience will be for the advancement of the Kingdom of God, and put their hands to it. They are not primarily motivated by position, power, or prestige. They will pursue a high-flying career if it advances the Kingdom most. They will give up their high-flying role and do something with little to no pay if that will advance the Kingdom most.

Discipleship and following God is the key to a transformed nation and a transformed world. I mean discipleship in the historic Christian faith. Teach people the truth of the Gospel. Teach them not just to recite the Creed but to live it, and you will change the world around them. Teach people to take the Bible seriously, to be open to the Holy Spirit, and to follow where God leads, and you will unleash a spiritual tidal wave of hope in your country. Show people that God really is big and His purposes really are magnificent and they really are part of His plan, and they will never be the same again.

Unbelievable? Yep. True? Absolutely.

This is the moment: Grasping a once-in-a-generation opportunity

There is a generation rising around us that won't settle for the status quo. They are hungry for a greater intimacy with God. They want to press ahead with what God wants. They are straining at the leash of our conservatism and comfortableness. They are the radical traditionalists, who, like Jesus, want to hold on to the truths of Who God is and what God does and press into the world around them with a message of hope.

You see it in the rise of student prayer movements. You see it in packed apologetics conferences for young people. You see it in the growth of student Christian movements. You see it in the explosion of worship, praise, discipleship, and hunger for spiritual encounter. I think there is a generation pushing into wider spheres of influence, and hungry to make a mark for God.

I don't think everyone in the Church is ready for the next twenty years. I think some churches will continue to decline. I think some denominations, in their rush for relevance and credibility, will commit missional suicide by losing their distinctiveness. I think some Churches will put Jesus alongside other options. I think some Christians will give up on the idea of being different from society. And I think they will gain popularity for a few years and then discover that they have lost their power and direction.

But I think others will grasp the moment. They will grapple with the Bible. They will lay themselves on the altar for God. They'll commit to holding up the name of Jesus. They'll preach and live the truths of the Creed.

They will hold out the hope of a Father to a fatherless generation.

They will offer the forgiveness of the Son to a broken and damaged society.

They will share the power of the Spirit with those who feel locked out.

They will point people back to the God of the Scriptures, whose heart breaks with compassion and whose hands are stretched out in invitation.

They will rebuild ancient ruins and become restorers of streets with dwellings as they live out their faith, take the risk, and dare to believe that change is possible.

God is at work in the world.

As unbelievable as it might sound to you, the Gospel still works. We don't need to panic. We don't need to be fazed by the scepticism that is around us.

Our society doesn't need us to be perfect, but it does need us to be authentic. This Gospel is still changing lives. What our society needs more than anything is a band of Christians who actually believe this stuff.

We can be confident that God has not finished with us yet. We can be confident in the Bible. We can be confident in the Lord Jesus. We can be confident in the resurrection. People are still searching. They are still thirsty and they are still hungry.

Christ is still the answer.

It's not over yet.

Are you up for the adventure of a lifetime?

As unbelievable as it might sound to you, God needs you.

He invites you to join His family, to follow His ways, and to change the world.

Unbelievable!

About the author

The Revd Malcolm Duncan is Senior Pastor at Gold Hill Baptist Church, Chalfont St Peter. He is Chair of the Spring Harvest Planning Team and author of a number of books including *Kingdom Come* and *Risk Takers*.

Connect with Malcolm Duncan:
On Twitter via @malcolmjduncan
On Facebook via Malcolm Duncan

By the same author and published by Monarch:

Kingdom Come: The Local Church as a Catalyst for Social Change
A book exploring the vision and role of the local Church in society.

Risk Takers: Living as God Intended
A book exploring the opportunities and challenges of living a Christ-centred life today.